# Ukraine's
# Revolutionary Ghosts

# Ukraine's Revolutionary Ghosts

☙

*Nikolas Kozloff*

ISBN: 1523413123
ISBN 13: 9781523413126

# Voyage to Ukraine

To THE EXTENT THAT U.S. media covers Ukraine at all, outlets tend to focus on "what's good" for "the west" and how "we" can outflank Vladimir Putin. Going overboard with the geopolitical analysis, the media invites wonky policy insiders to discuss how "U.S. interests" should be deployed in the fight to protect Kiev. Since the vast majority of Americans have little or no say over what their government does, it's unclear who the policy wonks are actually referring to when they casually employ such terminology. On CNN and even the supposedly liberal-leaning MSNBC, John McCain is routinely consulted on how the Obama administration has made "us" weak and failed to stand up to Russia. Speaking with CNN host Candy Crowley, McCain said Russia was a "gas station masquerading as a country," and suggested that there were a host of measures that "we" and our European friends could take to rein in Putin's foreign policy maneuvers.

Just what do Ukrainians themselves think about politics and the wider war with Russian-backed separatists? From watching the talking heads on CNN, you wouldn't really know. Anton Shekhovtsov, a visiting fellow at the Institute of Human Sciences in Vienna and an expert on Ukrainian politics, told me in an interview that "Western media tends to deprive Ukrainians of any agency of their own. There's always a lot of talk about conflicting interests between the west and Russia, geopolitics and expansionist interests on both sides. All of these issues are certainly legitimate, but somehow Ukrainians themselves get left out of the discussion." Denis Pilash, who has worked as an activist in a variety of different groups including socialist Left Opposition and a student labor union called Direct Action, agreed. In the west, he told me, many so-called experts refuse to see Ukraine as an independent player, but rather as a mere object or "bargaining chip."

In an effort to get away from such stale policy discussions, I conducted a research trip to Ukraine in late 2014 where I interviewed experts as well as activists who had participated in the Maidan revolution. With all the media frenzy centering upon hostilities in Ukraine, it's easy to lose track of Maidan and its original goals. By now we've all heard the official version of events: concerned lest the government of Viktor Yanukovych tilt Ukraine toward the Kremlin, demonstrators occupied Maidan square in Kiev and pushed for a so-called association agreement with the European Union. Once security forces resorted to repression, however, the crowd became radicalized as some activists called for an end to the overall culture of corruption. As violence spiraled out of control and Yanukovych was eventually forced to flee the country, there was little doubt that peaceful demonstrations had morphed into full-scale rebellion.

Just what were protests in Kiev all about? It's a somewhat tricky question since rebellion against Yanukovych unfolded in distinct phases with constituencies often pushing conflicting agendas. But while the crowd at Maidan may have held differing notions about social change, most were united in calling for more transparency and accountability in government. Indeed, many sought to rid Ukraine not only of Yanukovych but also the country's "oligarchic" interests. Hoping to move protests in a more progressive direction, young leftist activists injected an element of such anti-oligarchic politics on the Maidan. The independent left, however, developed a much more far-reaching "anti-authoritarian" critique extending beyond the mere confines of cronyism and oligarchic rule. Just because one opposes pro-Kremlin sentiment and Putin's designs on Ukraine does not necessarily mean the European Union is a paragon of social and economic justice. To their credit, many Ukrainian leftist activists opposed Yanukovych while also remaining steadfastly critical of the west including NATO expansion and the International Monetary Fund's plans to institute economic austerity.

Speaking with Maidan political veterans proved to be a sobering experience. While the revolution in Kiev has achieved some limited goals and reforms, much of the anti-authoritarian spirit of the square has dissipated. Paralyzed with fear over the war and Putin's earlier annexation of Crimea, most Ukrainians have placed their trust in Petro Poroshenko, a member of the country's oligarchic elite. As hostilities smolder in the east, the public has tended to focus on military developments rather than pushing for Maidan's earlier political agenda. And while the Maidan had its own progressive social component, street protests also gave rise to worrying rightist and nationalist sentiment. Needless to say, the government has failed to provide sufficient criticism of the far right and may even seek to legitimate such undesirable elements in the long-term. In the wake of revolution and the midst of war, Ukrainian politics is becoming increasingly more volatile. Intent on proving their anti-establishment *bona fides*, public figures are turning to firebrand populism in an effort to bolster their own "authenticity" and folksiness.

The wrenching experience of revolution and war has prompted some soul searching in Ukraine, as the new nation seeks to explore its own identity, historical icons and symbolism. It is to be hoped that Ukraine adopts and embraces multiculturalism and a pluralistic ethos, while facing down retrograde forces which have come to the fore in recent years. While in Ukraine, I discussed the issue of ethnic relations and minorities with local observers, and this booklet touches on the status of Jews, Tatars, Gypsies and others. For me, the question of ethnicity carries key personal significance since my grandfather grew up in the town of Pereyaslav, located just outside of Kiev. During my visit to Ukraine, I made sure to visit Pereyaslav in an effort to grapple with complex historical relations between Jews and Ukrainians. Other chapters in the booklet further explore the post-Maidan *milieu* and deal with such topics as the role of women, the LGBT community and conservative values as represented by the church and traditional religion.

This booklet is a distillation of dozens of online articles published on al-Jazeera and the Huffington Post, representing the culmination of nearly two years of intense research and thought. When I originally started to write about Ukraine, the topic represented a political as well as a geographic departure for me. Throughout my academic and writing career, I had focused on Latin America and the rise of the political left throughout the hemisphere. Disillusioned with recent developments there, however, I decided to turn to other areas of the globe in the hopes of learning more about idealistic movements abroad. To my chagrin, I observed how some ideological leftist writers in the U.S. viewed Ukraine through their own narrow-minded prism which tends to absolve the likes of Putin or others who challenge Washington. In line with such predilections, these writers tended to dismiss Maidan as a U.S.-supported movement with rightist undertones.

Though the downing of Malaysia flight 17 delayed my trip to Ukraine, I managed to fly into Kiev in late 2014. By the time I managed to get there, however, demonstrators had already left Maidan square and much of the public focus had shifted to the low-intensity conflict in the east with Russian-backed separatists. As a result, the mood seemed much more somber and austere than the heady idealistic days associated with Yanukovych's departure. Nevertheless, I was still curious about the long-lasting political legacy at Maidan. Whilst in Ukraine, I approached independent political activists on the left, not to be confused with the old Soviet left, to get their own feedback on such matters. They too seemed disappointed with the mainstream media portrayal of their country, let alone left ideologues in the U.S. who failed to pay any attention to new progressive elements on the Maidan.

In seeking out potential interviews, my thinking was informed by the following question: "What will it take to create a more progressive and tolerant country in the midst of war?" It's doubtful whether economic or political elites, along with their "oligarch" backers, are interested in such an agenda, let alone the far right nationalist set. To be sure, the independent left in Ukraine is a numerically small portion of the population. On the other hand, activists on the left circuit have played an important role at different strategic points, and it is to be hoped that their progressive agenda will ultimately prevail. Some Ukrainian nationalists have written to complain that my list of interviewees isn't "comprehensive" enough, whatever that means, or that I must be a propagandist in the service of Vladimir Putin, or furthermore that I shouldn't criticize Kiev in the midst of war. In my defense, I simply state that

I had my own priorities in Ukraine and tried to do the most exhaustive job I could under the circumstances. Needless to say, Putin's lavish payouts failed to pay for a sampling of local caviar.

In addition to providing fodder for wide-ranging political and historical debates, this booklet contains dozens of photographs which I took during my stay in Kiev and Pereyaslav. Though the capital is hundreds of miles from the separatist war in the east, patriotic displays were evident on the streets. Indeed, the Ukrainian national colors of yellow and blue could be seen all over Kiev, and I have digitally enhanced the colors to give a sense of potent political symbolism. In contrast to images depicting riots and political violence on Maidan square, my photo essay may seem reflective; arriving in the wake of the revolt against Yanukovych, I found Maidan rather somber and empty. Peer a little harder, however, and one may glimpse mementoes to fallen martyrs of Maidan which reflect political and even religious undertones of recent conflict. On another part of the square, I encountered a kind of makeshift museum consisting of placards depicting heroic struggle. In the wake of revolution, the spot became a popular tourist destination as Ukrainians sought to get a handle on the meaning of their rebellion as well as an incipient sense of national identity.

# CHAPTER 1

# EuroMaidan and the Independent Left

WHILE IT'S PERFECTLY CLEAR THAT John McCain and other right wing hawks represent a political danger, and could even inflame age old Cold War tensions, it's no less true that Putin is engaged in a naked power play in Ukraine and Crimea. Why can't one criticize both Washington's foreign policy machinations while also decrying Putin's excesses? Adopting such a position seems clear as day, yet some leftist commentators cannot seem to get beyond the narrow confines of their own ideological fixations. According to such writers, the Kremlin has stood up to U.S. imperialism and thus Putin's opponents must be on the wrong side of history.

Needless to say, such rigid positions lead to dismay amongst actual left activists on the ground in Kiev who have nothing to do with U.S. maneuvering or Kremlin adventures for that matter. What is the current status of the independent left within Ukraine, and how much staying power does it have? Academic expert Shekhovtsov is somewhat skeptical. "Politically," he told me, "such forces are not very viable or competitive in elections. There are some left wing/liberal forces which I would call progressive, but we're not talking about political parties but rather clubs, *milieus* or circles around particular magazines." The expert added "I don't think the left can oppose right wing nationalism. Their share of the vote [if you subtract the old Communist Party of Ukraine, which isn't even that Communist but more pro-Russian] is smaller than the political right's. I think the only force which can counter right wing extremism is the mainstream political center."

Nevertheless, the independent left has played an important oppositional role at crucial times. Activist Pilash, who is a post graduate student at Kiev National University, remarked in conversation, "It's worrying that some Western leftists view Putin as 'anti-imperialist' while he carries out an adventurous intervention in Crimea and our comrades from the Russian left (members of Russia's Socialist Movement, Left Front, anarchists and anti-fascists) are being persecuted and jailed by his regime." Pilash added that it was time for western activists to start organizing a peace movement which would mirror the earlier yet short-lived anti-Iraq war protests of 2003. This time, however, activists should advance a more nuanced critique as anti-war forces must oppose not only Washington's foreign policy but also Russian aggression.

According to Pilash, independent left activists confront a variety of different adversaries and a challenging political *milieu*. All Ukrainian parties, Pilash added, are essentially rightist and favor a "neo-liberal" economic agenda. At the same time, parties are socially conservative and do their utmost to steer political unrest away from progressive values. Trade unions meanwhile are weak, while the local Communist Party pushes a mixture of Pan-Slavism and "nostalgic Stalinism." Pilash said newer but small leftist groups had arisen to challenge the *status quo*. In addition to Left Opposition and Direct Action, other outfits include the Autonomous Workers' Union, which is anarchist in orientation, and some feminists, environmentalists and anti-fascists. During Maidan protests, these forces organized a hospital guard which helped protect injured protesters from the police. Unfortunately, far right fascists attacked and brutally beat up three trade unionists during demonstrations.

## MAIDAN STUDENT GENERATION

Mention student activism in the United States or Europe, and some may conjure up pictures of firebrand leftists, intent on disrupting business as usual.

In Ukraine, however, that is not always the case. Rector of Kyiv Mohyla academy Serhiy Kvit has remarked that "European students are better at communicating with other protest groups, their actions are much more radical, and their protest actions engage many more participants. The victories of Ukrainian students are due to the fragility of the government rather than the strength of a well-organized movement." The nature of Maidan student protest during the first few weeks may lend support to such views. At this early stage, student protesters tended to be liberal and merely pro-European Union. Foremost in the minds of many was the Ukrainian educational system: would local universities keep pace with modern and efficient standards if Yanukovych failed to sign a so-called association agreement with the European Union? Could universities attract top talent and professors from foreign institutions if the president continued his pro-Kremlin tilt away from Europe? And lastly, would Ukrainian students have the ability to travel and work abroad?

On the surface at least, the association agreement with Europe was appealing to many students, though the initiative proved somewhat thorny for leftists. The latter, in fact, feared the agreement might lead to greater austerity cuts under western-style institutions like the International Monetary Fund (I.M.F.). Vadym Gud, a veteran of Direct Action student labor union, was immersed in such controversies at the time. Within the group, Gud remarked, "We had a huge debate about getting involved in the protests." Most leftists, he says, didn't like the idea of signing a trade pact with the European Union. Gud, who espoused "socialist, anti-authoritarian" politics at the time, nevertheless took a more pro-E.U. line. Perhaps, he reasoned, Ukrainian activists could help to move the E.U. to the political left in the event that Kiev signed an association agreement with the west.

As it turned out, Gud was not alone. Pilash, too, noted the ironies confronting the student left. "I was skeptical about the Maidan protests from the very outset," he told me. Though he participated in the Maidan movement, Pilash does not share the mainstream's "triumphalist" narrative about the overall course of events. To be sure, Pilash and his colleagues did their utmost to inject a bit of radical politics at Maidan square. They distributed leaflets, for example, calling for improved healthcare and education and a ban on offshore money laundering. From the very outset, however, Pilash held a "very pessimistic outlook" about the potential for meaningful social change. During his own political evolution, Pilash had focused more on social questions like poverty, inequality and police brutality rather than foreign policy issues such as Yanukovych's tilt toward Russia and away from the E.U. At the time, Pilash said, "some Greek left colleagues wrote me and said, 'You're crazy, you want to be in the European Union even as we are burning the E.U. flag?'"

Natalia Neshevets, another young activist with Direct Action, told me that leftist students were few in number; "maybe in the hundreds." Despite low turnout, she and her colleagues sought to inject progressive values into incipient protest. "My friends and I did not agree with the E.U. association agreement," she remarked. "We tried to talk with people about our own vision for Europe. Will the future just be about the free market, or will it be based on free transportation, free education and human rights?" Neshevets added, "We not only wanted to change faces in power but the inherent power structure itself. We hoped to get away from leaders and promote more genuine, democratic participation." In line with such thinking, Neshevets and fellow activists formed democratic decision-making assemblies on the Maidan.

## Initial Skepticism

Pilash and Neshevets weren't alone in feeling skeptical. Take for example Denis Gorbach, another political activist who helped co-found Autonomous Workers' Union, an outfit which aims to organize industrial laborers in the workplace along anarcho-syndicalist lines. The group models itself after the American I.W.W. or Industrial Workers' of the World ("Wobblies") and the union is comprised of former students, IT specialists, journalists, artists, designers and a few workers. Gorbach estimates that the group, which is based in Kiev and the eastern city of Kharkiv, has about 40 members. When protests erupted on Maidan, Gorbach and his outfit initially refrained from participating. In the first few weeks, the activist adds, most of the demonstrations consisted of mere pro-European Union students and liberals. "We were very skeptical," Gorbach remarked, "because at the beginning, in November 2013, the whole movement was merely intent on making president Yanukovych sign a trade pact with the European Union."

Serene and tranquil scenes on the Maidan were rudely interrupted when riot police attacked student protesters and removed activists from the square. The crackdown quickly led to political radicalization and sparked protests against police brutality. Students began to shift away from their previous emphasis on the E.U. and started to call for improved educational policies and an end to police crackdowns. Before November, Gud explained, "No one contemplated the overthrow of the government," but afterwards "everything changed and Maidan started to focus on the removal of government at the very least." Yegor Stadny, another veteran of political protest on the Maidan, added that at this point "We started to think about systemic change. Students realized that merely shaking up top figureheads wouldn't result in wider societal change."

By January, 2014 Gorbach began to sense a palpable change in crowd dynamics. As parliament became increasingly dictatorial, it became clear that Maidan had less to do with rival trade pacts or individual politicians like Yanukovych and more to do with an overall struggle "about individual freedoms and individual rights." From this point onwards, there was no turning back: for Gorbach, Maidan became "a choice between a more repressive Yanukovych tied increasingly to the Kremlin; or the demonstrators who weren't exactly our political ideal though certainly more progressive than the government." Down at Maidan square, some of Gorbach's colleagues participated in protests while sustaining severe injuries. The activist adds that his group "received a considerable influx of people who hadn't been political up to that point."

Pilash, too, was becoming less skeptical. On the Maidan, he told me, it was common to hear people chanting "all politicians out!" The grassroots, it seemed, had become more anti-establishment. Many protesters, Pilash added, started to become radicalized and to call for punitive measures against Ukrainian oligarchs and the powerful. For example, demonstrators sought to put an end to the corrupt and incestuous alliance between business and government. Moreover, they also sought to shed light on privatization initiatives so as to reveal the true extent of what had been stolen. In quick order, activists launched student strikes in Kiev and demanded the release of colleagues who had been imprisoned. Hardly in the mood for compromise, Yanukovych passed a set of draconian laws in January which granted impunity to police officers who had violently put down the protesters. Amidst worsening violence on the square, Gud set up an information team and a Facebook page dedicated to "revolutionary struggle" which quickly attracted a whopping 300,000 followers. Gud also conducted live online reports from the front lines, where protesters hurled Molotov cocktails and government snipers responded in turn with live ammunition.

## CLASS DYNAMICS ON THE MAIDAN

At this point, Maidan might have become more radical by pushing a truly transcendent social agenda. Unfortunately, Gorbach told me, the movement was hindered by internal frictions and a lack of long-term vision. To be sure, the working class, including office and industrial laborers, "was obviously dominant" at Maidan. On the other hand, even though the working class was numerically important, it didn't steer developments on the ground. Though trade union leaders sought to play a role, such moves weren't backed up by the rank and file. That's not too surprising, Gorbach added, since "the regular trade union movement is extremely weak and almost non-existent" in Ukraine.

In the midst of political confusion, Gorbach said, "it was difficult to say who was actually in control" on the Maidan. For its part, the opposition took to the stage and politicians sought to "put on the brakes and steer things as they saw fit." The working class might have taken advantage of the circumstances by pushing harder for its own agenda, but progressive forces instead chose to pursue limited short-term goals and ally with business oligarchs. Maidan became a multi-class movement, united in its desire to merely get rid of Yanukovych.

Progressive elements also lacked cohesive self-organization. "As I see it," Gorbach said, "people were acting as individuals in the crowd. They were unable to establish a decision-making mechanism like they did at Occupy." To be sure the crowd did establish a kind of archaic, medieval decision-making body which encouraged people to elect leaders by shouting or even throwing their hats into the air. That's a "very primitive understanding of democracy, which is fine for the twelfth century but not for the twenty first," Gorbach remarked in a drole aside.

Initially at least, Pilash said many on the Maidan were receptive to a left-ist social agenda, though over time "you saw a lot less of this kind of rhetoric," and such ideas were entirely lost amidst all the "mainstream, pro-market neo-liberal politics." In addition, the crowd stopped being assertive in its demands while losing a sense of momentum, solidarity and unity. "When protests ended," Pilash declared, "ordinary people weren't involved in making decisions anymore and left such tasks to the establishment." In the wake of Poroshenko's electoral victory, civil society retreated and "there was very little political engagement."

If anything, however, developments in the wake of Maidan proved the need for a strong and independent left. Political elites seemed intent on pursuing radical deregulation, including cuts in energy subsidies and public expenditure. Meanwhile, the government pushed privatization and "liberalization" of the labor market. *Fiscal Times* writes, "since we detest euphemisms here, this means hire 'em-fire 'em will be the new rule." Finally, "a health-insurance system of unspecified structure will be introduced and public spending on education will be determined on the basis of merit." For the technocrats, this all sounds great but "if you are a housewife, a student, or a steamfitter, this might just as rationally sound like somebody's idea of hell."

## STUDENT IMPACT

Having been radicalized, students refused to demobilize once Yanukovych fled the country. In February, activists occupied the Ministry of Education and demanded not only improved higher education standards but also appointment of a new minister who would push innovative policies. "Some Direct Action members took part in the occupation of the Ministry of Education," says Neshevets. "We went in there and locked all the doors." Eventually Serhiy Kvit, rector of Kyiv Mohyla academy, was appointed minister in the new government and met approval by students. Kvit immediately committed to a "road map" of educational reform including increased accountability and transparency. "The Ministry of Education put all its finances up on the web site so you could verify that," Neshevets explained proudly. In addition, universities were granted more autonomy and professors became subject to assessment standards.

In defiance of the government, which wants to raise the pension age and increase working hours, Ukrainian left activists have demanded the lowering of retirement age, extending vacation time and shortening the work week. Meanwhile, even as authorities move to raise the price of metro and bus fares, activists have called for free public transport in Kiev. One group, Left Opposition, wants to move away from a presidential system in favor of a parliamentary republic where executive power is greatly curtailed. Activists have also called for nationalization of industry; the creation of independent workers' unions; introduction of a luxury tax; prohibition on offshore capital transfers, and access to free education and healthcare amongst other demands. The leftist student movement in Ukraine has certainly had its ebb and flow over the last couple of years. In the wake of Maidan, what's next for the younger generation? "Things have tilted so far to the right that disillusionment is inevitable," says Pilash. Pausing for effect, the activist muses, "I don't think this last Maidan was the last."

In the wake of protests, Maidan was turned into a kind of makeshift shrine and museum as the nation sought to figure out the lasting meaning of revolution. Above, a love poem written by noted Ukrainian poet, dissident and journalist Vasyl Symonenko. The writer's verse satirized the Soviet regime, and during the 1960s and 70s his work was suppressed by the Communist Party.

# CHAPTER 2

# Disillusionment and War

AMIDST INCREASING HOSTILITIES IN UKRAINE, many social aims of the Maidan revolution could be lost or simply forgotten. Indeed, activists expressed dismay that war with Russian separatists in the east of the country had served to distract attention from urgent social reform, including the need for progressive taxation and redistribution of wealth. What is more, the war has literally siphoned off experienced political veterans. Activist Neshevets, in fact, explained that a few anarchists had enlisted in volunteer units and gone off to fight the rebels. "I am totally against fighting in this conflict," Neshevets remarked, "and it's strange for me when leftists take on patriotic positions." Nevertheless, she added, "some activists see the war as a protective measure in response to direct Russian aggression." Most activists who enlisted were men, Neshevets declared, and they defended their decision by arguing that it's important to stand with common folk and not just be "elitists."

Without diminishing student accomplishments on the Maidan, it's difficult to say the young generation has succeeded in fundamentally altering the underlying fabric of society. Speaking with Neshevets in a local Kiev cafe, the young activist states that students held more far-reaching goals than simple education reform. Despite these shortcomings, Neshevets added that smaller victories on the educational front represent a necessary first step. For his part, former student activist Stadny remained somewhat disappointed by the course of events. "I don't think students aimed to bring the current government into power," he explained. Every political party, he added, had recruited veteran protesters from Maidan, including right-wing paramilitaries. "For me this is like…really?" he told me. In an ironic chuckle, Stadny asked rhetorically, "We fought on Maidan just to allow these right-wing people to form their own political parties and achieve representation?"

Walk around the Maidan, and one would be forgiven for thinking the square was ever home to massive civil unrest. To the contrary, most people including youth seem focused on shopping at neighborhood chain stores within the vicinity. In this sense, students might not be so different psychologically from the post-Soviet masses. "Young people build their notions about society around consumerist ideas," Stadny remarked. "This is really sad --- there is no more idealism."

Around Maidan, consumerism is rampant.

Around Maidan, it's back to normal as people jump
into the subway after finishing work.

As if students didn't face enough challenges already, the war against Russian separatists has also derailed or postponed wider notions of social justice. Pilash said that one of his student friends had undergone an "existential crisis" which led him to sign up for the military. When the young man returned from combat, "he told all kinds of stories about post-traumatic stress disorder, people going crazy, rape, and crimes on both sides." Yet another environmentalist colleague witnessed the killing of a friend during government protests on the Maidan. The man "then went on a kind of anti-Russian crusade" and enlisted in a volunteer battalion. Pilash explained that his contact had been taken prisoner and he and his peers had no idea when the environmentalist would be freed.

It's not all such a dark and violent picture, however. Rather than rush to war, some other veterans of struggle have used their skills to push for a progressive agenda. Stadny remarked that Maidan struggle had encouraged more people to get involved with local non-governmental organizations or NGOs. Stadny, who works as a higher education policy analyst at Kiev's Center for Society Research, said that working for an NGO might be more "fruitful" than simply jumping into the political arena. Unfortunately, he added, "a lot of journalists and activists went into politics and we lost them as well as our voice."

At the very least, NGO's can be effective in monitoring government. Failing that, Stadny argued that "if you want to have any influence you should join the government and start working in a ministry. For me, simply running for office and becoming a member of parliament is more about PR. About eighty percent of what gets done in society is the result of government ministries; not politicians. While parliament passes laws, government is ultimately responsible for implementation."

Like Stadny, Gud also works on the NGO circuit, in this case Kiev's Center of United Actions. There, he is affiliated with the group's parliamentary division which is helping to monitor Ukrainian MP's. "We look at where they get their money; their corruption cases and so on," Gud remarks. To be sure, he added, the left debates whether it should be involved in issues like corruption, "which is generally more of a liberal concern." Nevertheless, Gud said there were plenty of leftists working at his organization and during his free time, the Direct Action veteran "wears an activist hat."

## Nationalism and War

If anything, the war with Kremlin-supported separatists has made it even more difficult to question Ukrainian nationalism. People have been speaking more Ukrainian, notes Tetiana Bezruk of the Congress of National Communities of Ukraine. In a local Kiev café, Bezruk told me that it has become important to demonstrate one's patriotism in school. The researcher adds that in some, but not all, public elementary schools children sing the national anthem more than before. "It all forms part of this cute patriotism," she said, "where you supposedly love your country so much that you are willing to sing the anthem several times a day."

To be sure, patriotic surges are unsurprising in light of war. The question, however, is whether the current government has gone too far in seeking to appease the nationalist right. In light of recent developments, there's some evidence that Poroshenko has done exactly that. Indeed, according to human rights activists the president has provided a Ukrainian passport to a Belarusian neo-Nazi. The man, Serhiy Korotkykh, served as a fighter in the eastern conflict zone and helped to defend Donetsk airport from Russian separatists.

During a ceremony, Poroshenko awarded a medal to Korotkykh and praised the Belarusian as "courageous and selfless." Experts however claimed that Korotkykh was a founder of a neo-Nazi group in Russia and pointed out that the Belarusian had been charged for involvement in a Moscow bombing. For good measure, Korotkykh was also detained in Minsk for allegedly stabbing an anti-fascist organizer. Though top Ukrainian authorities have rejected the claims as defamatory, such developments send a chill through the left activist community which feels increasingly vulnerable and beleaguered.

Mementos to the fallen martyrs proliferate around Maidan,
even as many ponder what was gained.

CHAPTER 3

# Oligarchs and Populists

⚘

IN THE MIDST OF WAR and heightened nationalism in Ukraine, many demonstrators who participated in protests at Maidan Square have been gripped with a profound sense of shock and disillusionment. During the revolt against Yanukovych, the crowd called for a thorough overhaul of elite corruption, cronyism and the incestuous business-government revolving door. Yet, if anything, recent developments have only served to bolster tycoons (commonly referred to in Ukraine as "oligarchs") and their position, thus torpedoing hopes that Maidan might have led to a more level and socially equitable playing field.

For Ukrainians, corruption is one of the most pressing problems facing society. According to the *Economist*, "weak institutions, low morale, and an underdeveloped sense of public service have made everyone from judges to traffic police liable to corruption over Ukraine's entire post-Soviet history." Recently, Transparency International categorized Ukraine as one of the most corrupt countries in the world. In the study, Ukraine ranked only slightly higher than Congo, Angola and Haiti. Needless to say, Ukraine is reportedly the most corrupt country in Europe, even more so than Russia. Janek Lasocki, an advocacy coordinator at the European Council on Foreign Relations, notes "By way of illustration, one can point to the oft-repeated statistic that Poland and Ukraine were similarly run and sized economies in 1990; and yet today Poland's economy is three times larger."

These stark realities have prompted the likes of Devin Ackles to sit up and take notice. Ackles, who works as an analyst for CASE Ukraine, a not-for-profit specializing in economic research, has remarked that "Ukraine has become one of the biggest kleptocracies in the world." In a telling article, the expert succinctly sums up Ukraine's plight. "Shortly after independence in 1991," he writes, "a new tradition developed in Ukraine. People entered the government, whether at the local or national level, primarily to find ways to improve their financial standing by milking the system. When MP's turn up to work in Range Rovers while sporting fancy tailor made suits and unfathomably expensive timepieces, no one is fooled for a second that they were able to pay for these luxuries on their meager state salaries." During this time, so-called "oligarchs" benefited handily from shady privatization deals under President Leonid Kuchma. Ukrainians must endure corruption in their daily lives, ranging from "small, almost unperceivable bribes given to doctors to ensure slightly better care or the crippling bribes that businesses have to hand over in order to make sure they will not be subject to a raid by the tax inspection police."

## A Kleptocratic "Mafia"

In light of such history, it's hardly surprising that protesters would display a decidedly anti-corruption tint at Maidan. Indeed, while rampant abuse and cronyism characterized much of the go-go 1990s, corruption reached incredible new heights under Yanukovych. In a move reminiscent of the mafia, the president created a group called "the Family" which siphoned off rents from Ukraine's many economic sectors and institutions. In a spiral to the bottom, Yanukovych bought off police, judges and even electoral officials. It is estimated that a whopping $1 billion was siphoned off every year through sheer abuse of public procurement tenders. Summing up the overall political mood of the era, the *Economist* remarks, "The runaway corruption of Mr. Yanukovych's rule—and the cynicism that it symbolized—was one of the motors of the Maidan protests that toppled him from power."

In the wake of Yanukovych's fall, the new government in Kiev carried out a number of high profile arrests, seized property and put the former president's house on show, which included an ostrich zoo and a vintage car collection no less. In short order, Kiev passed a raft of anti-corruption laws and even created a new investigative body called the National Corruption Bureau. In an effort to rein in shell companies and hidden financial interests, all enterprises except for state-owned entities were required to open their books and disclose who, precisely, benefited from their business. Meanwhile, a reform group comprised of experts and activists managed to pass laws designed to change the process of public procurement, which is reportedly a huge source of corruption. Under the new system, the process will be opened up and subject to scrutiny, while state purchases linked to connections on tender committees will be halted. In another win for reform advocates, access to information on salaries and benefits of state employees will be publicized.

In the fight against corruption, politicians declare that foreigners may be more trustworthy than local Ukrainians. Poroshenko in fact has called for the appointment of foreigners to head the new anti-corruption bureau. Hoping to reassure jittery western investors in the *Wall Street Journal* no less, Poroshenko boasted of his new cabinet, including a former U.S. citizen at the helm of the Ministry of Finance; a Lithuanian at the Ministry of Economic Development and Trade, and a Georgian tapped to oversee Ukraine's health system. Corruption, Poroshenko remarked, was a "tumor" which had sapped the Ukrainian economy for far too long. Indeed, analysts claim that Ukraine's kleptocracy has prompted western investors to take flight and abandon Ukraine. "The new approach of hiring foreign professionals," Poroshenko continued, "will be practiced throughout the government. We are welcoming representatives of other nations, from the private and public sectors, who are experienced with enacting reforms in their own countries and are ready to accept Ukrainian citizenship."

Even as the government moves to promote foreigners, it has cracked down on allegedly questionable Ukrainians. Under the so-called law on lustration, former members of the Communist Party, KGB, Komsomol (communist youth league) and those who previously served under Yanukovych have been excluded from office. The legislation is designed to promote more accountability within the state apparatus. On the surface at least, the law sounds like a positive development, though conveniently legislation failed to apply to Poroshenko himself, nor to most officials currently elected to office. That would seem somewhat inconsistent, since Poroshenko previously served as Yanukovych's trade minister. Moreover, in the words of the *Economist*, the current oligarch president made a large fortune through "opaque deal-making" in the 1990s. In other respects, the law on lustration has been labeled "murky and overly sweeping" and has the "potential for political score-settling." Somewhat ominously, radical protesters have already conducted their own vigilante-style justice by throwing supposedly corrupt politicians into trash bins and even beating them. Reportedly, law enforcement has failed to halt such incidents.

One can only hope that reform efforts will succeed, but there are severe reasons to doubt that corruption will be curtailed. Ukraine in fact has long possessed anti-corruption measures, but the state has repeatedly failed to halt cronyism. By the time Yanukovych fled the country, he and his cronies had allegedly siphoned off billion of dollars, thus leaving Kiev in a *de facto* state of bankruptcy. As a result of such depleted finances, Russia found it easier to take advantage of Ukraine through its annexation of Crimea and separatist war. Furthermore, questions still remain about the incipient National Corruption Bureau: some have pointed out that the entity is solely dependent on state revenue, and as a result the agency could be "subject to the whims of those in power" and mere vicissitudes of the moment. Even more blatantly, Ukraine's Lithuanian Minister of Economic Development and Trade recently resigned his post, claiming that overwhelming corruption had made his job untenable. The minister's resignation was greeted with shock and disillusionment within the foreign investor community.

## OLIGARCHS AND WAR

As if Poroshenko himself wasn't proof enough of oligarchic rule, one need look no further than Igor Kolomoisky, an economic magnate who was appointed to run the region of Dnipropetrovsk near conflict-ridden Donetsk.

Kolomoisky is worth approximately $1.6 billion and has reportedly conducted business deals for twenty years under successive administrations. Lasocki of the European Council on Foreign Relations has remarked, "in exchange for keeping his province stable and defended from separatists, [Kolomoisky] has had his businesses interests left untouched."

Even as oligarchs plunder the state budget, ordinary Ukrainians are left to fend for themselves and living standards have stagnated. It's politically challenging, however, to question the oligarchs in the midst of war. When asked if he thought politicians intentionally focused on war as a means of deflecting attention from the need for greater transparency, Vadym Gud of Center UA hardly bats an eyelash, remarking "yes, sure." Oligarchs like Koloimoisky have wrapped themselves in the flag so as to pre-empt unwelcome criticism of their business dealings. In fact, the oligarch has even funded the Dnipro Battalion, a paramilitary outfit. By funding pro-Kiev groups fighting in the east, Kolomoisky performed wonders for his own public relations brand. "These bands of half-trained volunteer warriors," writes the *New Yorker* magazine, have done much of the fighting in the current conflict, operating largely independently of the government, and often without adequate coordination."

One may ask: why has the Ukrainian war effort been so haphazardly organized? According to the *New Yorker*, the Ministry of Defense is notoriously corrupt and can't be trusted with state money. In another passage worth quoting at length, the magazine adds, "The Western press often portrays Ukraine's volunteer-led war effort as a feel-good story of solidarity and ingenuity. But behind this volunteerism is a state whose institutions are so dysfunctional that they cause more harm than good. The state's failures could have dangerous consequences. The Maidan movement, Poroshenko, and those in favor of arming Ukraine have referred, again and again, to Ukraine's commitment to 'European values.' But a country full of privately funded battalions looks more like pre-modern Europe than like a potential E.U. member."

Just what kind of impact has corruption exerted upon the overall course of war? Recently, U.S. Vice President Joe Biden reportedly warned Poroshenko that corruption could prompt western backers to withdraw their support from Ukraine. Indeed, western allies might find it difficult to justify arms shipments when a large proportion of materiel simply winds up on the black market. In a sign of the times, NATO has created five trust funds to finance reform of the Ukrainian military even though soldiers don't have uniforms, let alone adequate food. "Trust funds?" *Fiscal Times* asks rhetorically. "NATO members, it turns out, are so wary of the Ukrainian command that they refuse to provide money directly." Surveying the political landscape, *Kyiv Post* remarks rather aptly, "The West has stepped on the rake of Ukrainian corruption one too many times to be fooled again. Ukraine should not get more billions in loans or millions more in aid until it changes."

## OLIGARCHS DERAIL MAIDAN REVOLUTION

The ascendance of Poroshenko is a bitter pill for activists to swallow. A chocolate magnate worth a whopping $1.3 billion, Poroshenko owns Ukraine's TV Kanal 5 and has assets in real estate, insurance and banking. Hardly afraid to throw his weight around, the oligarch has donated money to MP's and makes use of his TV station to push his own agenda. A living testament to the revolving door, Poroshenko made his way up as a businessman but later served as trade minister under Yanukovych himself. When his boss fell out of favor, the "King of Chocolate" enhanced his public standing by making a 180-degree turn and siding with protesters on the Maidan. In this sense, Poroshenko proved more flexible and independent than other oligarchs who preferred to stay out of the power struggle.

Nevertheless, *Foreign Policy* magazine writes that Poroshenko "probably would have never risen to his current position had it not been for the lack of credible leaders among the revolutionaries." In his rise to the top, Poroshenko also benefited from sheer political vicissitudes of the moment. When Russia banned products of Poroshenko's Roshen candy company, the Ukrainian public rallied to the homegrown oligarch and Poroshenko's credibility amongst voters was solidified. Scared and panicked amid hostilities with Moscow, Ukraine rallied to Poroshenko on election night and the oligarch spearheaded his own bloc in parliament.

Though perhaps the most prominent oligarch, Poroshenko is joined by a host of other tycoons. Many oligarchs are invested in the industrial east of the country, home to Soviet-era mines and factories. Most of the magnates, notes *Foreign Policy* magazine, "amassed their wealth by exploiting their closeness to those in power rather than through efficient management." In the words of the *New York Times*, "the ultra-wealthy industrialists wield such power in Ukraine that they form what amounts to a shadow government, with empires of steel and coal, telecoms and media, and armies of workers." By securing positions in government for themselves or buying off politicians, oligarchs obtain valued political influence. Through purchase of media outlets, oligarchs hope to forestall or preempt efforts to undermine their position.

Unfortunately for the oligarchs, Yanukovych began to squeeze the elites and promote his own group, nicknamed the "Family." Forced to compete against such incestuous interests, and leery of Yanukovych's plans to move Ukraine closer into Russian orbit, oligarchs began to splinter. To be sure, most of the oligarchs' exports, which emanate from outdated and outmoded factories, were directed toward Russia. On the other hand, the oligarchs feared jeopardizing Ukraine's ties to the west, as well their easy access to fancy vacation homes and London's financial center. With the exception of Poroshenko, the oligarchs chose to remain neutral in the end --- unwilling to support Maidan protesters but equally wary of Yanukovych's pro-Kremlin crackdown. Once Yanukovych ceased to be useful, the oligarchs simply abandoned him. Without key top-level support, the president was forced into exile and today, in the wake of Maidan, oligarchs are nervously looking around, wondering what the new shakeup in Kiev will mean for them. The safe bet is that plutocrats will try to play ball with government because making waves would be bad for business. Reportedly, the oligarchs have been "hedging their bets politically" in hopes of securing a kind of comfortable *status quo* in which their assets will be protected. At the very least, oligarchs no longer have to worry about the sinister sounding "Family," which imploded in the midst of Yanukovych's fall from power. The government meanwhile has been afraid of taking on oligarchic interests too intensely, since tycoons control eighty to eighty five percent of overall GDP. The oligarchs, activist Pilash told me, "are still in power. Maidan showed we could challenge politics, but economically we have the same guys in charge."

## Appeasing the Oligarchs

On the other hand, Kiev has officially at least taken activists' concerns seriously. In fact, Poroshenko has been engaged in a raft of anti-corruption initiatives designed to forestall the power of "rent-seeking oligarchs." The president has been under the gun, since western financial assistance is contingent on Kiev enacting reforms designed to curtail the tycoons' power. In the short-run, oligarchs too may wish to cooperate with reform since the specter of the International Monetary Fund withholding funds could torpedo the Ukrainian economy, and that in turn would harm their interests.

Despite these developments, grassroots activists may have a battle on their hands. Poroshenko himself has been dogged by corruption allegations in the past and has ties to one Dmytro Firtash, another oligarch who faces bribery charges in the U.S. In 2014, the magnate was arrested in Vienna at the request of the F.B.I., and Washington has charged the oligarch with violations of the Foreign Corrupt Practices Act. A grand jury meanwhile has ruled that Firtash, a gas, banking and minerals magnate, paid bribes to secure titanium for one of his U.S. affiliates. After being hauled into a local police station, Firtash agreed to post bail to the tune of $190 million (such a whopping sum may seem crippling but for a gas oligarch whose net worth may be more than $10 billion, the payment was a mere drop in the bucket).

From Vienna, the oligarch has loudly proclaimed his innocence while arguing that his entrepreneurial spirit is vital to Ukraine. Recently, an Austrian judge rebuffed Washington's extradition request and so the magnate is free to travel. Reportedly, however, Firtash abandoned plans to return to Ukraine after Kiev announced it would arrest him at the airport. Indeed, Ukrainian officials allege that the oligarch has long siphoned off massive amounts of Ukraine's wealth through gas-trading schemes. In a strongly worded editorial,

*Kyiv Post* remarks that Firtash should stay away from Ukraine as the "nation is better off without him."

Despite his political connections, Firtash finds himself in a difficult bind. In light of the oligarch's previous ties to Yanukovych, not to mention links to Russia's reviled Gazprom, the native son may find it difficult to recruit influential allies. Nevertheless, Firtash remains a power-broker and is hedging his bets, even from afar. Indeed, he and other oligarchs such as Rhinat Akhmetov are behind the so-called Opposition Bloc, an anti-Poroshenko political party. Even though Firtash represents the old guard oligarchy around Yanukoych, Poroshenko can't afford to alienate this larger than life figure. As a result, Poroshenko himself has sought to curry favor with the gas and minerals magnate. Just before the presidential election, Ukraine's Chocolate King flew to Austria to meet with Firtash. Reportedly, Poroshenko was eager to garner his fellow oligarch's support, and in particular to secure favorable media coverage on Inter, Firtash's own TV channel.

As if the task for reformers could get no more challenging, other oligarchs like Akhmetov add to overall political complexities. A steel magnate with a deluxe penthouse home in London, Akhmetov owns a business empire consisting of mobile phone companies, banks, real estate and even a media company. In Donetsk, he has interests in heavy industry, coal mines and metallurgy, and is considered by some to be the "de facto ruler of Donbass." A tycoon worth a staggering $12.5 billion, Akhmetov has --- in the words of the *Guardian* --- "smoothed over an early reputation for mixing with tough street operators." Nevertheless, some reports suggest the oligarch acquired his wealth during the "lawless early 1990s." When Akhmetov's mentor, an alleged mobster, was killed in an enigmatic bombing, the Donetsk metal king inherited a huge financial empire. Though investigative journalists have sought to link Akhmetov to the shadowy underworld, the oligarch steadfastly denies such charges and has even sued over the allegations, all the while claiming he simply made some fortuitous and lucky gambles over the course of his business career.

Akhmetov is currently down but not yet out of the game, and the oligarch could still exert an impact on Ukrainian political life. During the Yanukovych era, the oligarch was a key supporter of the disgraced president as well as his political organization, the Party of Regions. In a leaked cable published by whistle-blowing outfit WikiLeaks, U.S. ambassador to Ukraine John Herbst refers to the Party of Regions as a "haven for Donetsk-based mobsters and oligarchs" and names Akhmetov as a "godfather" of the Donetsk clan. According to an article in Vice media, Akhmetov "is reported to have used a system of patronage to exert considerable influence over several deputies in the house," and the oligarch's businesses "flourished exponentially." Another piece in *Der Spiegel* adds that Akhmetov --- along with key ally Firtash --- controlled about half of Yanukovych's party between them. Indeed, the magazine adds, the two tycoons controlled their country's political scene "as though it were a business joint venture."

Political unrest on the Maidan placed Akhmetov in a quandary. When demonstrations occurred, *Spiegel* notes, both Firtash and Akhmetov "began to distance themselves" from Yanukovych. "It was clear to both of them," the article adds, "that if worse comes to worst, and the West imposed sanctions on Ukraine, their businesses would be the first to be affected." When confrontations turned bloody, "both Akhmetov's and Firtash's TV stations changed their coverage of Independence Square: Suddenly the two channels, Ukraina and Inter, were reporting objectively on the opposition. The message of the oligarchs was clear: We're letting Yanukovych fall." For Akhmetov, the demise of Yanukovych raised the unsettling possibility that the new government might investigate oligarchic interests. Because he had so many assets in Ukraine, Akhmetov did not flee to Russia in the wake of Maidan, along with Yanukovych and his cronies. Reportedly, however, Poroshenko has Akhmetov "in his crosshairs" and the authorities are trying to break up monopolies while reversing "rigged" privatizations of state-run enterprises. Indeed, lawmakers seek a probe of Akhmetov's iron ore assets, purchased under earlier privatizations. According to analysts, Akhmetov acquired the assets for a fraction of their true worth.

Within this arcane and Byzantine political *milieu*, who wins or loses? On the surface at least, the removal or at least eclipse of Firtash and Akhmetov seems to suggest a popular victory for reformers and the spirit of Maidan.

However, a power vacuum has led to the rise of yet more oligarchs who are keen to take advantage of political and economic opportunity. Take, for example, Igor Kolomoisky, an oligarch with a net worth of about $1.6 billion who reportedly likes to feed sharks in his own office aquarium as a favorite pastime. An oil and banking magnate, Kolomoisky gained a reputation during the early 2000s as a "corporate bandit" after carrying out hostile takeovers. Vice media reports that such tactics gained the oligarch and his business partner the familiar nickname of "The Raiders." At least some of the takeovers, the publication notes, "were physically enforced." In one case, hired hands reportedly wielded "baseball bats, iron bars, chainsaws, and rubber bullet pistols" which proved useful in securing ownership over a local steel plant. In addition to his other assets, Kolomoisky has invested in the prominent 1+1 Media Group, which controls eight Ukrainian television channels.

"Over the past two decades," notes *Foreign Policy* magazine, Kolomoisky "has always found a way to cooperate with whoever ruled over the country." Yanukovych, for instance, allowed the oligarch to maintain a stake in the state oil company. Unlike Firtash and Akhmetov, however, Kolomoisky proved more flexible once protests hit the Maidan. Kolomoisky in fact offered political support to demonstrators on his television channel, and he later emerged as a winner in the Kiev power reshuffle. Needless to say, Kolomoisky wasted no time in taking on his oligarch competitors, and 1+1 TV channel ran an inflammatory report on Firtash claiming the oligarch was a Kremlin puppet. Hardly deterred, Firtash struck back in turn by seeking to blacken Kolomoisky's reputation on Inter.

Perhaps mindful of rising star Kolomoisky, the Poroshenko government appointed the oligarch as governor of Dnipropetrovsk near conflict-ridden Donetsk. *Tablet* magazine notes, "Many Ukrainians assume that he had taken up the position mostly to protect his myriad business interests from being expropriated by the new regime." In the short-term, Poroshenko certainly benefited from having a powerful oligarch on his side, but in the long run the president may be wary of magnates' growing power. "Kolomoisky is certainly poised to capitalize on the current weakness of the central government," *Foreign Policy* noted in 2014, and "many

Ukrainians are eagerly casting about for a strong leader, and for some it's Kolomoisky who fits the bill." Last year, a jittery Poroshenko sacked Kolomoisky from his position as governor of Dnipropetrovsk. Reportedly, the president "had no choice" in the matter when Kolomoisky literally deployed his own personal militia in an effort to block Kiev from regulating his financial interests.

## WILD WEST OF POPULIST POLITICS

How will the Ukrainian public respond to oligarchs in the not too distant future? On the one hand, many Ukrainians admire Poroshenko and trust him to protect the country in a time of peril. On the other hand, the spirit of Maidan could turn against the president if he is perceived as going soft on oligarchs. Within such a polarizing political *milieu*, as well as deep economic malaise which has plagued the country, it is possible that a certain strand of anti-oligarchic populism could flourish. "Promising to combat the oligarchs," notes *Foreign Policy* magazine, "is a popular demand among nearly all Ukrainian voters, from the liberal left to the nationalist right." Andreas Umland, a professor of European Studies at Kyiv-Mohyla Academy, told the publication that the surge in populism underscores an underlying "helplessness and despair." "The established parties," he remarked, "don't seem to have the answer to dealing with Russia and the separatists. So, many want to see new faces and tough approaches."

One key figure exemplifying the new firebrand spirit is Oleh Lyashko of the Radical Party. Largely unknown before Ukraine's recent political troubles, Lyashko has since rocketed to fame. Indeed, the politician came in third during Ukraine's presidential election with eight percent of the vote, and the Radical Party scored 22 seats in the 2014 parliamentary election. Poroshenko needs to attract coalition partners to maintain a majority, and Lyashko has signaled that he might be willing to strike a deal. Whether or not Lyashko can sustain his party in the long-term is unclear, though for now the populist has been somewhat successful in maneuvering through his country's political landscape. Like many of his competitors Lyashko favors closer European integration, though he has separated himself from the pack by fusing such pledges with folksy, anti-oligarchic populism.

In addition, Lyashko has benefited from the decline of other rightist and nationalist groups such as Svoboda or Freedom Party, which has had difficulty finding its footing in the post-Maidan *milieu*. Indeed, during a recent parliamentary election, Svoboda failed to attain the 5 percent threshold necessary to pick up seats. Oleksandr Zaytsev, a historian at Lviv's Catholic University, says the party's days may be numbered. During Maidan protests, he remarked in an e-mail, public perceptions of Svoboda plummeted and "the most radical party figures were hissed and driven from the podium during rallies in the western Ukrainian city of Lviv." Zaytsev adds that Svoboda officials have "become odious figures in the eyes of many Lviv inhabitants."

A high-flying ultra-nationalist who charters private flights around Ukraine, Lyashko has developed a loyal following amongst anti-Russian young men. The combative populist employs incendiary and bombastic rhetoric whilst labeling his opponents "traitors." Responding to the country's existential crisis, Lyashko frequently dons military fatigues and is known for his many appearances on TV talk shows. The *New York Times* notes that Lyashko "has the knack for self-promotion of a radio shock jock. He has dumped a truckload of potatoes outside the prime minister's office in support of Ukrainian farmers [and] tried to bring a cow into Parliament for a point about rural land rights." Moreover, Lyashko found himself in the midst of a physical brawl in parliament no less. When a lawmaker accused the populist of traveling to the eastern conflict zone as a mere PR stunt, Lyashko charged that his colleague had ignored adverse conditions faced by Ukrainian soldiers. "Look at this pot-bellied fatty," the macho Lyashko declared. "Instead of going to the Donbass and helping our guys, people like him go to parliament and raise their hands." Heated rhetoric prompted Lyashko's opponent to promptly hit the populist in the face.

Sometimes Lyashko's antics can veer into ominous territory. The populist has led vigilante-style squads into eastern Ukraine in an effort to capture rebel leaders and humiliate them in front of the camera. In one case, Lyashko captured the so-called Defense Minister of Donetsk People's Republic. In the back of a car, the populist proceeded to interrogate the man, who was clad solely in boxer shorts. In a video, Lyashko accused the man --- who displayed cuts on his arms and legs --- of being a traitor and a terrorist. In another case, Lyaskho accused a local police chief of being a collaborator and then asked, "Should I shoot you now or later?" Needless to say, human rights groups say Lyashko's tactics amount to kidnapping. Furthermore, the notion that Lyashko might embrace progressive populism is belied by his support for infamous Azov Battalion, a volunteer brigade fighting Russian separatists in the east. The outfit espouses far right nationalism, and is reportedly run by an extremist patriot group which considers Jews and other ethnic minorities to be "sub-human." The Azov Battalion has called for a white Christian crusade against such minorities, and sports Nazi symbols on its insignia.

## Oligarchs and Populists

Like other populists, Lyashko has been careful to project a kind of "common man" image. Though he is university educated, Lyashko speaks simplified and colloquial Ukrainian which he admits to playing up for effect. "Why do people support me?" he asks rhetorically. "Because they see that I'm the same as they are," he said. "This is a secret of our ratings, because you need to communicate with people in a way they will understand." Lyashko added, "My performance might look plainer, maybe primitive to some point. Better I be a populist than to be the authorities who are desperately different from people, and don't understand people's problems and how to solve them." In the search for authenticity, Lyashko has adopted the three-pronged Ukrainian pitch fork, a traditional symbol of peasant protest. The instrument underscores Lyashko's desire to jab at his opponents and rid the country of oligarchic influence. At political rallies, Lyaskho's rural supporters frequently carry such farming equipment. The populist views country folk as his principle base of support in opposition to big business and the oligarchs. Unlike other politicians, Lyashko claims that his electoral campaigns are mostly funded through small donations.

Whether Lyashko is really anti-establishment in practice is subject to debate, however. Critics have accused him of lambasting oligarchs while simultaneously taking campaign donations from tycoons. Meanwhile, the populist has been a frequent guest on Inter TV channel, which is owned by anti-Poroshenko oligarch Dmytro Firtash. Perhaps, Lyashko has simply opt-ed to ally with certain oligarchic interests while conveniently criticizing oth-ers. The populist has favored nationalizing oil and gas businesses owned by Kolomoisky, an oligarch whose 1+1 Media group launched an investigation into Lyashko's holdings. The report showed that the populist enjoyed a lav-ish lifestyle including Mercedes, private jet and luxurious private home. It's unclear what's behind such tit-for-tat feuding and murky oligarchic politics, but it does seem Lyaskho has cultivated some powerful enemies. Reportedly, the state security service has warned him of a planned assassination plot. "Ukrainian oligarchs have ordered my killing," declares Lyashko, accusing Kolomoisky of personally seeking his liquidation.

Kolomoisky hasn't commented on the allegations, but his deputy regu-larly attacks Lyashko on Facebook, accusing the populist of being a "fighting faggot." Rumors about Lyashko's homosexuality go back some time, and have apparently hit home. "Homosexuality," notes the *New York Times,* is "not well tolerated in Ukrainian society." According to academic scholars Andreas Umland and Anton Shekhovtsov, homosexuality is essentially taboo and may even spell political poison in post-Maidan Ukraine. The authors note that the radical right is distinguished by "social conservatism, heterosexism, and populist nationalism." It was "ethno-nationalism," the authors declare, which helped to build up political cohesiveness at the Maidan and foster a broad alliance "from the radical left to the extreme right." Sensitive to allegations which might undermine his macho image, Lyashko has bent over backward to refute claims pertaining to his personal life. Indeed, the populist posted a Facebook photo of himself appearing shirtless in a romantic pose with his wife, and on TV he has even judged women's breasts no less.

Like other populists, Lyaskho's ideology is difficult to pin down. Historically, the politician has stood up for small business, higher pensions and social benefits. He meanwhile supports so-called "radical reforms" including an end to government corruption and greater taxes on the wealthy. On the military front, the populist would like Ukraine to join NATO and, somewhat improbably, to undertake nuclear rearmament. Lyashko also wants his country to join the E.U. but opposes heavy borrowing from the International Monetary Fund (I.M.F.). "The wish list is long," notes the *New York Times*, "with few explanations of how to afford or accomplish it." How do we explain the political success of Lyashko, who up until fairly recently hadn't achieved much notoriety? Populism, academic expert Shekhovtsov explained to me, means offering "simple solutions to complex problems. It's more of a rhetorical style than a set of beliefs. Lyaskho himself has no ideology. People are frightened because of the war and they feel helpless in the face of Russian aggression. As a result, they find comfort in Lyashko's simplistic slogans."

Needless to say, some on the independent left circuit view the emergence of populism with raised eyebrows. Lyashko, says activist Pilash, "speaks as if he's this guy who tells the truth with lots of nationalist rhetoric." On the other hand, Pilash added, the firebrand politician isn't so unique because in Ukraine "there's no clear division between populists and the establishment," and to a greater or lesser extent all domestic politics lacks coherent ideology. Moreover, populism may derail popular struggle and Maidan's aspirational goals. Pilash explained that the mere term "populism" can serve as a convenient foil for political elites. "When you say anything about real social needs you are labeled a populist," the activist declared. "If you're for free education you're a populist. If you say 'power to the people,' you are labeled a populist. 'Direct democracy' and you are labeled a populist."

# CHAPTER 4
# Rise of the Far Right

⚘

FOR SOME TIME, THE POLITICAL right in Ukraine has been gaining visibility. That, at least, is the impression I get after speaking with local activists on the independent left circuit in Kiev. Pilash, who participated in anti-Yanukovych protests, told me he first came into contact with the hard right long before Maidan. "All the trouble started when rightists started targeting blacks, even though there were very few of them here in Ukraine," Pilash said. He added that far right Svoboda tried to stir up "anti-migrant hysteria" by holding rallies. Moreover, the party sought to halt immigration and reserve civil service positions for "ethnic Ukrainians." In 2006, Pilash attended a punk rock concert in Kiev and witnessed Nazi skinheads attacking an Azeri man. He and his friends flew to the aid of the gentleman, which prompted the rightists to angrily turn against them.

According to academic expert Shekhovtsov, Svoboda has exhibited several ideological strands, "including anti-communism, anti-liberalism, racism, anti-Russian sentiments, glorification of Ukrainian historical right-wing extremism and fascism." In 2012, the party garnered more than 10% of the vote in parliamentary elections. Svoboda espouses many traditional and retrograde views, and has argued that religious affiliation and ethnicity should be listed on official identity documents. Socially conservative, Svoboda has also sought an end to abortion in Ukraine. The party has glorified Ukrainian partisans from World War II and brandishes rightist flags. On the surface at least Svoboda sounds rather consistent politically, though Bezruk of the Congress of National Communities of Ukraine believes the party is ideologically inchoate in certain respects. A researcher writing her thesis on Svoboda, Bezruk says the party isn't right wing precisely but more populist in orientation. Svoboda pretends it is nationalist but favors European integration. "How do you reconcile such a strange contradiction?" I ask. "Exactly," Bezruk chimes in.

Perhaps, the far right realized that its anti-immigrant messaging had been only modestly successful in Ukraine and so it changed course by opposing anarchists, feminists, and the LGBT community. According to the BBC, "ultranationalists, and their extreme right fringe," were "a small part of the overall campaign - a subgroup of a minority" during Maidan protests. Nevertheless, for its small numbers the right has "played an outsized, though not decisive, role." Furthermore, "Euromaidan's political heads have at various points seemed unable, unwilling or even afraid to rein in the radical right." The BBC adds that many EuroMaidan supporters "bristle at, or deny, any claim that the movement contains an influential ultra-nationalist element, fearful this will be used to tar the entire movement…they simply call them 'patriots.'"

At a certain point during Maidan, Pilash began to feel a little politically uncomfortable. A native of the culturally diverse western Ukrainian region of Transcarpathia (also known as Ruthenia or Zakarpatts'ka Oblast'), Pilash has mixed ethnic roots. Over the course of protests, the activist observed many Ukrainians bellowing nationalist slogans such as "glory to the nation and death to enemies." Before Maidan, he says, "this slogan was only used by a couple of fringe right wing groups." On the square, however, a wider cross-section of people embraced the slogan. In the wake of Maidan, some leftist activists grew concerned the right might actually obtain real political power. Take, for example, Gorbach of Autonomous Workers' Union, who told me, "there was a dangerous point [at the end of February, 2014] when the entire governmental apparatus lay in ruins and the neo-Nazis were one of the few organized forces on the ground. So, that was kind of scary."

Fortunately, the right never took over the reins of power, though later Svoboda was incorporated into the new government and party members acquired various cabinet positions. Shortly thereafter, Svoboda suffered an electoral defeat in further parliamentary elections when the party failed to garner a 5% barrier to qualify. Nevertheless, the BBC notes that if far right parties had banded together and not splintered the vote, they might have qualified. The *Guardian* meanwhile notes "it is short-sighted and formalistic to conclude that the Ukrainian far right is insignificant based on the lack of electoral success. The rhetoric of many politicians which could be called centrist or even liberal has moved significantly to the right, competing for the increasingly patriotic and even nationalist voters." Leftists have grown increasingly concerned at the ominous air of impunity which has descended upon Ukraine. After Maidan protests ended, Pilash said, he was physically assaulted by a local right wing blogger. The man spotted Pilash on the street and beat the leftist activist while repeatedly shouting "communist!" Fortunately, Pilash managed to escape and wasn't severely injured.

## Far Right and Azov Battalion

Far from rejecting or repudiating such odious and questionable elements, the Ukrainian political establishment has moved to shore up the support of rightists fighting in volunteer battalions in the east. Take, for example, Poroshenko's coddling of Serhiy Korotkykh, a Belarusian and member of so-called Azov Battalion. According to the BBC, right wing nationalist Azov is run by extremists who consider Jews and other ethnic minorities to be "sub-human." The outfit has called for a white Christian crusade against such minorities, and sports Nazi symbols on its insignia. While Azov is only one of many volunteer groups fighting in the east, it has the backing of some top authorities in Ukraine.

Though figures like Korotkykh are promoted by official circles, the Ukrainian media is notoriously timid about taking on rightist politics. According to the BBC, prominent Ukrainian newspapers ask no controversial questions when interviewing notable right-wingers. One news agency even airbrushed out accusations of extremism when Poroshenko awarded a new passport to Korotkykh. "There are significant risks to this silence," notes the BBC. "Experts say the Azov Battalion, which has been widely reported on in the West, has damaged Ukraine's image and bolsters Russia's information campaign." Another infamous Azov commander is Andriy Biletsky, who has been promoted to the rank of lieutenant colonel in the police. The military figure has openly admitted that some men in his unit "are interested in their historical roots," though this may be difficult to understand for more modern, "uprooted" nations such as the United States. Biletsky moreover made no apology for his controversial military insignia, which he said harks back some 600 years in Ukrainian heraldry.

As the far right gains respectability in wider society, left activists watch with growing unease. When asked if he was concerned about the Azov battalion, Pilash remarked "Of course. These people attacked us even before the war and committed hate crimes. But now, they have real combat experience and have actually killed people. It's very dangerous when they return, and such fighters are glorified as heroes because they struggled for Ukraine and therefore one shouldn't question their loyalty or credentials. The mainstream has no real problem with these figures." There's no danger of the far right coming to power in Kiev, noted Gorbach, though in a long-term strategic sense rightists may hope to install a dictatorship once the war is over. For now, however, there's an alliance of convenience between Kiev authorities and far right groups.

In a report, the BBC sums up the situation in Ukraine quite succinctly. "The question of the presence of the far-right in Ukraine remains a highly sensitive issue, one which top officials and the media shy away from," notes the news outlet. "No-one wants to provide fuel to the Russian propaganda machine." Such "blanket denials," however, also hold dangers since this allows ultra-nationalists to "fly under the radar." The BBC adds, "neo-Nazis are indeed a fixture in Ukraine's new political landscape, albeit in small numbers. As a result, they have achieved a level of acceptance, even though most Ukrainians are unfamiliar with their actual beliefs. Ukraine's public is grossly under-informed about this. The question is, why doesn't anyone want to tell them?"

According to Pilash, rightists dress up in military-style outfits with red and black insignia and some paramilitaries are "linked to the most notorious figures in Svoboda." Pilash was particularly disturbed by one case in which Vasyl Cherepanyn, a lecturer at Kyiv-Mohyla Academy and editor of leftist *Political Critique* magazine, was brazenly attacked in broad daylight in crowded Kontraktova Square, right next to the university where he works. Cherepanyn was assaulted by a group of men dressed in camouflage paramilitary uniforms. As they proceeded to pummel their victim, the thugs shouted "communist" and "separatist." Unfortunately, police arrived late to the scene and failed to catch the assailants. For his part, Cherepanyn sustained heavy injuries including a fractured face. Pilash said the attackers had no clear insignia on their uniforms, but he suspects they may have been affiliated with local battalions assisting the police.

Poroshenko himself claims to be shocked and outraged by such violence, including a recent protest outside parliament. During the demonstration, which sought to oppose plans for greater autonomy in eastern separatist enclaves, someone apparently hurled a grenade. The explosion killed three members of the National Guard, left another officer in coma and wounded more than a whopping 140 people. Authorities blamed the explosion on a fighter in so-called Sich volunteer battalion, which has deployed to the eastern front and has ties to Svoboda. In Ukraine, "Sich" refers to historic Cossack homelands. Though Cossack is a loaded term and carries unpleasant historic meaning for some, nationalists recently revived the word by referring to a Maidan protest area in Kiev as a "Cossack Sich."

Rather questionably, the government itself has ties to the Sich battalion, which falls under the official control of the Ministry of the Interior. Despite such links, Poroshenko called the attack "an anti-Ukrainian action" and demanded that "all organizers, all representatives of political forces... must carry full responsibility." Svoboda on the other hand denies any responsibility and claims the authorities are out on a witch hunt to deface the party. Whatever the case, it's a little odd that the authorities have only now woken up to the ominous threat of right wing groups. Indeed, the attack in front of parliament followed close on the heels of another incident in south-west Ukraine, in which members of so-called "Right Sektor" battalion got into a shootout with local police.

As if such developments weren't concerning enough, Svoboda also has a peculiar habit of resuscitating dubious World War II icons. Party leaders admire "proto-Nazis" such as Ernst Jünger, and are "understanding" of Goebbels. They moreover talk about "purity of blood" and refer to Ukraine as "one race, one nation, one fatherland." Svoboda meanwhile idolizes the Ukrainian Insurgent Army or UPA, an outfit which fought against the Soviets in World War II but also collaborated with the Nazis at one point. During unrest at Maidan square, Svoboda brandished the traditional UPA flag. Rather provocatively, the party furthermore supports those who wish to display this particular flag at local soccer matches.

To make matters worse, Poroshenko has said the "timing is good" to define the status of the UPA, and the politician signed a decree establishing a "Day of Ukrainian Defenders" on October 14. The date is significant as it marks the anniversary of the UPA's founding. Taking to Twitter, Poroshenko added "UPA soldiers - an example of heroism and patriotism to Ukraine." What is more, Poroshenko has also praised Andrey Sheptytsky, a priest who worked in the Ukrainian Greek Catholic Church. Though Sheptytsky harbored some Jews during World War II, he initially supported the Nazis during their invasion of Ukraine, favored the UPA and endorsed the creation of a Ukrainian division within the Nazi SS. Very questionably, Poroshenko recently unveiled a monument to Sheptytsky in the western city of Lviv where Svoboda and the political right enjoy a degree of popularity. During a ceremony attended by 10,000 people, Poroshenko praised the priest.

## The Ricochet Effect

So just how is the independent left in Ukraine coping with the nationalist mood? According to activist Gorbach, civil society is "weak and atomized" and simply resigned to patriotism and nationalism. "Right now," he remarks, "if you protest the government you run the risk of being perceived as a [Russian] fifth column." In the wake of Maidan protests, Gorbach entertained hopes that demonstrations would continue and the public would reject neo-liberal economic austerity measures. Unfortunately, he remarked, "the war with Russia has negated such aspirations" by diverting valuable attention from social issues.

Aerial view of Maidan with adjacent memorial.

Former Maidan veteran Vadym Gud echoed such sentiments. Right wing battalions are on rotation, he remarked, and come back home periodically. Once, he remarks, he was attacked by street thugs in a café. Though the attack wasn't very serious --- Gud was punched from behind --- some of the activist's colleagues were attacked on the street and sent to hospital. The problem, he said, was that "most right wingers do not divide leftists into neat and separate groups. For them, everyone is Communist, Bolshevik and anti-Ukrainian. Therefore, 'you must be pro-Russian and we're coming after you.'" Like Gud, Neshevets is also concerned about right wing violence. During protests at Maidan square, rightist street thugs attacked activists, grabbing anarchist flags and crushing them. Neshevets says the attacks continued every day, yet the media failed to take the incidents seriously. "When we reported it," she says, "journalists would say 'oh it's just your left-right clashes, we're not interested in that.'"

If anything, Maidan has only served to bring the far right out of the shadows. Though still rather numerically small, rightists played a visible role on Maidan square where they brandished red and black UPA flags. Unfortunately, Poroshenko has passed laws which would make it illegal to express "public contempt" against UPA veterans. Dozens of scholars specializing in Ukraine protested the measures, remarking that the legislation would make it "a crime to question the legitimacy of an organization (UPA) that slaughtered tens of thousands of Poles in one of the most heinous acts of ethnic cleansing in the history of Ukraine." Bolstered by such mainstream support, the far right has become emboldened. On the eastern front, one volunteer unit fighting Russian-backed separatists calls itself the OUN or Organization of Ukrainian Nationalists Battalion. During World War II, the previous OUN allegedly committed an anti-Jewish pogrom in western Ukraine with the support of Nazi Germany._Needless to say, the Ukrainian Diaspora has reportedly supported rightist volunteer battalions whilst offering up historic wartime apologetics.

Predictably, such antics have hardly helped Ukraine in the court of public opinion. The OSCE (or Organization for Security and Cooperation in Europe) has grown concerned about the Ukrainian far right. Recently, the group expressed alarm after local politicians declared they would set up a monument to Stepan Bandera in the western Ukrainian city of Lviv. Bandera, a controversial historical figure, sought to make Ukraine into a one-party fascist dictatorship free of other ethnic minorities. Within the historical context of the 1930s, this primarily meant forcible removal of Poles from Ukrainian territory. Though Bandera was an anti-Soviet fighter, his followers were nevertheless tarnished with Nazi collaboration during World War II. If left unchecked, such failures to confront the past could jeopardize or damage relations with Western European countries which are intent on doing business with an ostensibly modern partner.

# CHAPTER 5

# Ukraine and Anti-Semitism Debate

༄

IN THE MIDST OF WAR and revolution, Ukraine is struggling to define its own national identity. Under such circumstances, the debate over anti-Semitism and political parties such as Svoboda assume central importance. Svoboda, whose leaders have made anti-Semitic remarks, has sought to reserve civil service jobs for ethnic Ukrainians and claims Stepan Bandera as a mentor. On the other hand, if recent political trends are any indication, anti-Semitic sentiment doesn't seem to be resonating much within Ukrainian civil society. Indeed, Svoboda failed to attain the 5% threshold necessary to pick up seats in one recent parliamentary election. Observers said the election was the first in which no political party played on anti-Semitism. Buoyed by developments, Jewish leaders felt encouraged and hoped Ukraine would continue along a tolerant trajectory. While such trends are positive, Jews still carry painful memories from their long history of oppression at the hands of local authorities. During the late nineteenth and early twentieth century, Jews were subject to a series of pogroms or attacks accompanied by destruction, looting, murder and rape. The fall of the Czarist Empire, however, hardly ameliorated further suffering. Indeed, during World War II, parts of the Ukrainian population collaborated with the Nazis in exterminating local Jews in occupied territory. In light of such dark history, how is the remaining 100,000-strong Jewish community faring in newly independent Ukraine with its renewed sense of nationalism?

When it comes to such questions, views can be somewhat nuanced. Josef Zissels, General Council Chairman of the Euro-Asian Jewish Congress, told me the threat of anti-Semitism has been greatly exaggerated. Confident that independent Ukraine had turned the page on its past, Zissels declared "When Ukrainians build a model for their future there is no place for anti-Semitism." To be sure, he concedes, there's some anti-Semitic sentiment at the lowest rungs of society, "but in the mainstream and the top there's no place for this type of thing." Zissels' office is located in Kiev's Podil neighborhood, a former trading and Jewish quarter which is full of picturesque shops and architecture. However, with the exception of a local *kitschy* Jewish restaurant, there isn't much tangible sign of Kiev's Jewish history. Despite their many historical contributions to Ukraine, Jews remain an enigma to many. Cyril Danilchenko, Zissels' personal assistant, says that when he tells other Ukrainians that he works for a Jewish organization they express curiosity. "They don't know much about Jewish culture," he said.

Shekhovtsov, my expert on the European far right, tends to concur with such views. In an interview, he expressed doubt that right wing nationalists would ever be successful in electoral terms. Moreover, he added, "I'm skeptical that Ukrainians would ever rally to a program aimed at 'ethnic cleansing' or the like." To be sure, he said, "it's sometimes very difficult to distinguish between civic and ethnic nationalism." Shekhovtsov was under the impression, however, "that in general nationalism tends to take on a patriotic rather than a xenophobic character" in Ukraine. "Though the EuroMaidan was oftentimes depicted in dark and ultra-nationalist colors," Shekhovtsov said, "the movement has spurred the growth of a civic nation. The myth of the 'heavenly hundred' has helped to contribute and consolidate such civic-mindedness and constitutional patriotism. I'm referring to the 100 or so martyrs at the Maidan who were shot and killed by riot police. Ukrainians died there, but also Russians, Poles, Georgians, an Armenian and a few Jews."

Back in Podil, Zissels poured cold water on the notion that Maidan represented some kind of backward or retrograde nationalism. "No, no, no," he said, shaking his head. "During Maidan," he declared, "we Jews and other ethnic minorities did not feel threatened by what was happening." Indeed, protesters on the Maidan created their own "Jewish Division" within local self-defense units. To be sure, Zissels conceded, right wing nationalists were visible at Maidan. However, he said, "they don't play a major role…and they aren't very numerically strong." When Yanukovych authorities tried to disperse protesters on Maidan Square, people formed self-defense units which had no links to right wing nationalists. At the end of January, 2014 Zissels estimates such units comprised some 15,000 people. At the time, nationalists affiliated with one group, Right Sektor, only numbered some 200 strong while Svoboda had just several hundred people under its banner.

Eyewitnesses tend to confirm Zissel's overall assessment of the political mood. Take, for example, activist Pilash who took part in Maidan protests. During demonstrations, he explained, "there was a Jewish klezmer band and the majority of people were fine with that." Pilash adds that many people consider Ukraine to be part of Europe and western values. Such forward-looking folk, he declared, "are eager to embrace Jews and other ethnic minorities." Nevertheless, the activist says "demonstrators were playing all kinds of bad nationalistic music on stage." Pilash guards against complacency and fears the political mainstream hasn't been sufficiently critical of the far right. Indeed, the activist said, stereotypes and jokes about Jews persist, and "there's always a certain tolerance for the right which could lead to resurgence."

## JEWS IN THE MIDST OF WAR

Bezruk, the researcher at Congress of National Communities of Ukraine, told me she was concerned about the rise of fascistic Azov Battalion which has battled separatists while employing symbols which are similar to those worn by Waffen SS units during World War II. "Azov Battalion is one of the biggest problems right now," she remarked. "People are very respectful toward anyone who is currently fighting, and it doesn't matter what your politics is."

While many Jews are undoubtedly perturbed by such developments, others are keen to prove their patriotism. Danilchenko, in fact, reports that many of his Jewish acquaintances took part in Maidan demonstrations. Jews took pride in the revolt against Yanukovych, he points out, and "some of them [even] adopted nationalistic symbols on their Facebook pages like the Ukrainian flag." Perhaps, the war may even serve to integrate Ukrainian Jews more fully into society. Danilchenko adds that local Jewish "oligarch" Igor Kolomoisky created volunteer battalions which took part in the war to the east. In media and political circles, Kolomoisky has typically been referred to as a power broker and his ethnic or religious identity is glossed over.

Some Jews, Zissels told me, have even served in the Ukrainian army. The expert adds that many Jews are driven by a visceral "phobia" toward Russia. In a bizarre twist, it also seems that a few Jews have even fought with far right Azov Battalion. According to Zissels, "Within Azov Battalion we have Nazis but also some Jews including individuals holding Israeli passports. They all call themselves brothers." When I express amazement and even incredulity at such developments, Zissels remarks "I speak to Jews affiliated with Azov Battalion regularly, and they do not report any anti-Semitism. For the time being these people are collaborating. After the war, when it ends, we will deal with local Nazis on our own terms."

## FIDDLER ON THE ROOF

My preconceptions about embattled minorities and right wing nationalism were again put to the test when I traveled to the town of Pereyaslav, located some 60 miles south of Kiev. The town was once home to Yiddish literary legend Shalom Aleichem (1859-1916) and the stage and film musical *Fiddler on the Roof* was based on the writer's stories. Iryna Kucherenko, director of the Shalom Aleichem museum, said the local Jewish community wasn't too concerned with right wing nationalism. Jewish women in Pereyaslav, she explained, had supported the Ukrainian war effort by helping to provide soldiers with appropriate body armor. Kucherenko added for good measure that a Jewish battalion had deployed to the front.

Despite its place in key literary history, Pereyaslav has failed to gain much cultural visibility. The local Sholem Aleichem museum is a decidedly modest affair, and the Jewish community has dwindled to a low of about 35 people, most of whom do not speak Yiddish. The museum itself is a recreation of the Yiddish writer's original house. Kucherenko explained that the interior, including décor and furniture, were all original. During a Rosh Hashanah ceremony, Jews of Pereyaslav celebrated Aleichem in a humble community center. Tsylya Meirovna Gechtman, a local historian, said the Germans executed members of her family during World War II, and even before the outbreak of hostilities many Jews had fled the town seeking greater economic opportunity and political freedom.

When asked whether Aleichem had received his just due in Ukrainian society, Kucherenko responded, "We are trying to get some attention from the Ministry of Culture, but Shalom must be raised higher because the level of recognition is inadequate." Historically, she added, the museum suffered from a policy of neglect and the premises had even been closed for a time. Perhaps that's not all too surprising: rather than celebrate cultural differences and museums off the beaten path, Kiev has a somewhat monolithic and static view of history. So says activist Pilash, who adds that Ukrainian history "is just based on the view of one ethnic group and nation building. It's all about Ukrainians, hardly anything about Jews and Crimean Tartars, Poles and Armenians."

Ukrainian nationalists might want to conduct some historical research so as to enhance cross-cultural understanding. According to Gechtman, Jews and Ukrainians lived in peace and harmony during Aleichem's day. There was no ghetto in Pereyaslav, and many native Ukrainians spoke Yiddish with their neighbors. Chiming in for good measure, Kucherenko adds that Jewish and Ukrainian life was "intertwined" and mixed marriages were encouraged. Moreover, though Pereyaslav was hardly free of political and social strife, most Jews achieved middle class status and Aleichem's family was hardly poor. Perhaps, Kucherenko and others will help to put Pereyaslav on the cultural map and thereby elicit more interest in long forgotten *shtetl* life. Recently, the Shalom Aleichem museum has become more popular, and Kucherenko hopes this will spur a Yiddish revival. "I myself am learning Yiddish at the moment," she declares enthusiastically.

Jews in Pereyaslav and elsewhere confront issues of identity within the new Ukraine.

A steeple in rural Pereyaslav.

## MALLEABLE IDENTITIES

To be sure I am interested in the Jewish perspective and local history, though I also have my own personal motivations for traveling to Pereyaslav. My grandfather Josef Kozloff (1890-1954) was born and grew up in the town and my family history elucidates many of the historical controversies which bedevil Ukraine to this day. The Kozloffs weren't impoverished, though life was difficult in Pereyaslav where the family worked in the local leather business and perhaps even engaged in some farming on the side. In an early photo taken in 1905, Josef and his brother Nathan pose for the camera. The two are dressed in their finest clothes, with Nathan sporting handsome boots and Josef wearing a traditional tunic. A young man intent on displaying cultured manners, Josef sits next to an inkwell holding a pen.

Joseph and Nathan Kozloff in Pereyaslav circa 1905.

Perhaps, many Jews feel relatively well integrated into Ukrainian society today but what about the longer historical record? Though it's unclear whether Josef spoke Ukrainian, he personally referred to himself as such. However, my grandfather lived in Pereyaslav during the Czarist period, prior to official Ukrainian independence. I never met Josef, who died before I was born. My father Max remarks that his family was "unfamiliar with cosmopolitan aspects" of life. However, Josef knew how to write and "took great pride in his beautiful penmanship." In the home, Josef spoke Yiddish though my grandfather was also quite proud of his literate Russian.

Kozloff leather factory in Pereyaslav.

From talking to local residents in Pereyaslav, I get the impression that ethnic identity took on a multi-faceted character during the Czarist period. Josef himself was imbued with a rebellious spirit which went against tradition. According to my father, Josef "was very anti-religious and secular. In this sense he was somewhat atypical." When Gechtman saw the old photo of Josef and Nathan, she exclaimed, "They are not wearing hats, and this is inappropriate for them. Jews are supposed to wear hats. Maybe they weren't Hassidic or Orthodox."

Imbued with an atheistic spirit, Jews such as my grandfather may have eschewed religion while embracing Russian language and literature. What is more, Kozloff itself is a Russian surname. According to Kucherenko, many Jews assumed such Russian last names and Czarist authorities encouraged mixed marriages. It was not uncommon, for example, to observe Ukrainian men marrying local Jewish women. Though officials never forced people to adopt Russian surnames, many Jews embraced the custom simply out of fear or concern they might fall prey to anti-Semitic attack or pogroms. However, if they were in a more trusting frame of mind, locals might also add their own Jewish name by writing it in brackets.

Another one of Josef's brothers, Julius or "Jitco" Kozloff

Though Jews were certainly subjected to anti-Semitism in Ukraine, it's not as if they were gripped with constant fear. According to Kucherenko, many Pereyaslav residents held stereotypical views about Jews but "there was no discrimination." Russian was the common language of daily business in town, though some villagers also spoke Ukrainian. It's also possible people communicated in a kind of pidgin called Surzhik, spoken by Jews to this day at the local community center. To hear Gechtman speak, Pereyaslav displayed a diverse ethnic complexion during Czarist times. At a local blacksmiths' shop, her own family employed a Ukrainian assistant who spoke Yiddish. At table meanwhile, her grandfather was fond of reading newspapers aloud in Russian to anyone who cared to listen. Indeed, within the household people were free to speak whatever language they pleased. Meanwhile, Jews were at liberty to work as tailors, blacksmiths, traders, shop owners, doctors, lawyers, teachers and even cab drivers.

Though Pereyaslav was tolerant in certain respects, the town was far from an ideal home for local Jews and many simply opted to emigrate. In 1910, my grandfather Josef and his family traveled to Chicago where they settled in a Jewish colony just south of the Loop. On an Ellis Island manifest, Josef Kozloff or Kozlow is listed as "farm laborer." An ambitious and entrepreneurial man, Josef took to his new adopted country with gusto, rarely discussing or reminiscing nostalgically about life back in the Old World.

It's not entirely clear why the Kozloffs chose to abandon Pereyaslav. The family certainly sought greater economic opportunities abroad. Yet, it's hard to believe politics did not play a role in the ultimate decision to leave. Would the Kozloffs and others have perceived Russia as the main threat to their existence, or rather rising Ukrainian nationalism? The question is somewhat complex, since Ukraine could be a tolerant place though such peace was punctuated by sporadic violence. In another complex twist, Jews and Ukrainians formed part of the Russian Czarist Empire at the time and both were subject to repression.

Jewish perceptions of Russia may have been nuanced. On the one hand, Josef seems to have regarded Russian language, music and history as a sign of high culture. On the other hand, many Jews reviled Czarist autocracy and repression within Ukraine. Alluding to the painful history of anti-Semitism, my father Max remarked, "I'm not sure if the family was victimized personally, but it would be hard to imagine Josef didn't witness something." In 1905, Russia was engulfed in a wave of political turbulence. In the midst of war with Japan, revolution and anti-Semitic pogroms, Josef and his brother Nathan distributed anti-Czarist materials and were arrested for subversion.

As Jews, meddling in such sensitive political matters took considerable courage. More non-Jews were engaged in political activities in Pereyaslav than Jews, Kucherenko says, since the latter were afraid of pogroms and retaliation. According to family lore, Josef and Nathan were caught and lined up to face a firing squad. For some reason, however, the execution was called off at the last minute and the brothers were spared. Still, however, there were other mortal dangers: young men were subjected to the draft though many resorted to extreme measures to avoid this fate. Nathan, for example, voluntarily tore his eardrum with hot metal so as to get out of military conscription.

## RUSSIANS, UKRAINIANS AND ANTI-SEMITIC VIOLENCE

As the governing authorities at the time, Russian czarist officials were most responsible for anti-Semitic violence. According to Kucherenko, state officials organized pogroms and did their utmost to blame Jews for stirring up political trouble. Attackers would enter Jewish households, damage windows and property and try to force people out. Yet despite high level tolerance of anti-Semitic violence, if not outright encouragement emanating from the upper echelons of the Russian government, some Ukrainians too seem to have played a role in local riots.

In 1905, pogroms broke out all over Ukraine including the largest cities such as Kiev and Odessa. According to the Jewish virtual library, more than 800 people were killed in ensuing violence. "The most prominent participants," notes one article, "were railway workers, small shopkeepers and craftsmen, and industrial workers. The peasants mainly joined in to loot property." It wasn't the first time anti-Semitic violence had swept through the region: in 1881, for example, Kiev's

Governor General turned a blind eye to severe anti-Semitic attacks. As violence spread, officials and police did nothing to restrain rioters.

Elsewhere, local Ukrainians took out their frustrations upon Jews, and "attackers came from among the rabble of the towns, the peasants, and the workers in industrial enterprises and the railroads." According to an article in the *International Encyclopedia of Social Sciences*, Ukrainian pogroms continued until 1884. Anti-Semitic attacks of the era were perpetrated mainly by migratory and railroad workers. The local population, however, *"passively observed the plunder and violence and left the mobs unhindered, seeing these pogroms against an unloved minority as a suitable release for the pressures of unresolved social issues* [my italics]."

Just where did my own family stand in relation to such history? From talking to local experts, I get the impression that inter-ethnic relations weren't so bad in Pereyaslav. I always wondered, however, why my grandfather chose to flee specifically in 1910. Speaking to Gechtman, I get some answers which help to clear up the mystery. In 1909, she tells me, Pereyaslav was engulfed in gang violence. One outfit, the *zelonyi* or green gang, named after a local warlord whose last name happened to be Green, robbed and murdered Jews in a series of pogroms.

As it turns out, the Kozloffs were fortunate to get out of Ukraine when they did. After my family departed, the plight of Jews became exponentially worse. With the outbreak of World War I, Ukraine witnessed tremendous political turbulence. In 1917, the Czarist regime fell and was replaced first by a provisional government and later by the more radical Bolsheviks. Ukraine then declared independence, which sparked a brief war with the Soviets. If that were not enough, Germans also occupied the country at the end of the conflict, and a costly civil war ensued. To this day, such turbulent history carries deep political meaning. Many Ukrainians look back on the civil war era nostalgically as a period in which they stood up to Moscow and the Soviets. The Ukrainian Diaspora, meanwhile, may extol nationalist struggle while demonizing Bolshevism. The question, however, is whether Ukraine demonstrated multi-ethnic tolerance during this key but chaotic period of history.

Initially, at least, local Jews seem to have regarded burgeoning Ukrainian nationalism with some approval. According to Yivo Institute for Jewish Research, Jews and Ukrainians collaborated for "both pragmatic and idealistic reasons" and sought to bring about a kind of post-revolutionary democracy. To their credit, Ukrainians pledged to extend individual Jewish and community rights, and even promised to make Yiddish into an official state language. Such "lofty ideals," however, were only shared by a "small circle of politically active Jews and Ukrainians in Kiev and major cities." As Yivo Institute writes, "The dominant experience of Jews in Ukraine during the civil war period was one of violence, as hordes of pogromists swept across the countryside. Various military organizations and independent hooligans killed tens of thousands of Jews in the worst violence ever experienced in the region to that time."

In light of the historical record, it is perverse that some Ukrainians champion this brief chapter of history. To be sure, all different kinds of forces were hostile to Jews during the Ukrainian civil war, from the anti-Soviet White Army to the Red Army. On the other hand, Yivo Institute writes that Ukrainian troops perpetrated the largest proportion of pogroms. According to scholars, so-called "Cossacks" allied to the Ukrainian government were involved in the attacks. Such developments are a little ironic since Ukrainian authorities had previously extended rights and privileges to the Jewish population. Apparently, however, the government was unable to control its own unruly troops and may have even turned a blind eye to abuses.

Today, Ukraine is making a big push to eradicate its Soviet past and recently, parliament even banned communist symbols and names. As part of the legislation, all monuments, place and street names associated with Lenin are to be removed. But while no one is excusing the excesses of totalitarian rule, Lenin has a better historical record in certain respects than Ukraine during the civil war. In fact, though the Red Army was guilty of some anti-Semitic violence toward the end of World War I, many Jews eventually joined the Soviet army as a means of collective self-defense.

Perhaps, Jews were favorably impressed with Lenin, a revolutionary who vehemently opposed anti-Semitism. According to Yivo Institute, "Jews flocked to join the Red Army in such numbers that a special section had to be set up to train these Yiddish-speaking youngsters who were probably holding a weapon for the first time in their lives." Suspecting the Jews were becoming increasingly pro-Soviet, pogromists went on the rampage and attacked Jewish communities in a vicious cycle to the bottom.

For Ukraine, a newly independent country, such debates carry deep political meaning and while the country is more tolerant of ethnic minorities than many other nations, Kiev ought to push for greater historical understanding. To this day, many embrace a kind of *kitschy* nationalism as well as highly problematic historical symbols such as the mythical Cossack. While the mere mention of Cossacks is enough to instill fear in the hearts of Jews, some Ukrainians seem completely oblivious to such controversies and become defensive when confronted with such criticism.

## WARTIME CONTROVERSY

In an effort to build up a more pluralistic and tolerant society, Ukraine might emphasize historical periods which were free of ethnic strife. Yet Kiev seems intent on squandering any international public support it might have had amidst a bizarre crackdown on free speech and censorship of controversial historical debates. Through its crackdown, Kiev has encouraged and furthered certain negative stereotypes about Ukraine rather than seeking to overturn old perceptions. At issue is Ukraine's contentious World War II past, some of which isn't particularly flattering. With the support of Nazi Germany, militias affiliated with the extremist Organization of Ukrainian Nationalists (OUN) allegedly committed a pogrom in the western city of Lviv.

Writing in the London *Independent*, journalist Patrick Cockburn notes that while "Ukrainian politicians and historians have denied complicity... surviving Jewish victims, other witnesses and contemporary photographs prove that Ukrainian militiamen and mobs of supporters carried out the pogrom, though the Germans oversaw it and committed many of the murders." One scholar, John-Paul Himka, has concluded that the pogrom was mostly conducted by the OUN under German supervision. According to Himka, the OUN sought to demonstrate to the Nazis "that it shared their anti-Jewish perspectives and that it was worthy to be entrusted with the formation of a Ukrainian state." While the OUN also fought the Soviets and strived for an independent Ukraine, many leaders were influenced and trained by Nazi Germany. Indeed, the OUN could be characterized as a far right terrorist group which hoped to consolidate an ethnically homogenous Ukraine and a totalitarian, one party state.

"The truth is that the official policy of the OUN was openly anti-Semitic, including approval for Nazi-style Jewish extermination," writes Eduard Dolinksy of the Ukrainian Jewish Committee. The OUN in fact played an important role in pogroms which spread across Western Ukraine in the summer of 1941, resulting in the deaths of tens of thousands of Jews. After the Nazis dissolved the militias, many members linked up with the Ukrainian police and helped carry out the Holocaust throughout Western Ukraine. Then, for good measure, the OUN assumed control over the Ukrainian Insurgent Army or UPA in 1943.

A paramilitary outfit, the UPA initially leaned toward Germany but later turned against both the Nazis and the Soviets. The *Times of Israel* notes "according to some historical accounts the group murdered thousands of Jews in the 1940s." Other historians, as well as supporters of the UPA, dispute this claim, arguing that many Jews themselves served in the ranks of the organization. A recent article by Reuters claims the UPA shuttled victims into labor camps where they were subsequently executed. Furthermore, it is claimed the UPA was guilty of conducting ethnic cleansing of Poles in 1943-44. The massacres in Eastern Galicia, which formed part of an overall UPA strategy aimed at creating a homogenous Ukrainian state, resulted in the deaths of 100,000 people.

Amidst smoldering war in the east with Russian-backed separatists, Ukraine desperately needs allies and popular foreign support. Yet strangely, political elites are running hard in the opposite direction in an effort to coddle the extremist right. At issue is a highly controversial law signed by Poroshenko which honors the OUN and UPA. Under new legislation, it would be a crime to question the likes of the UPA. Specifically, legislation stipulates that Ukrainians and even foreigners who "publicly insult" the memory of wartime partisans "will be held to account in accordance with Ukrainian law." Though certainly distressing, Kiev's approval of the retrograde law comes as little surprise: former President Viktor Yushchenko, in fact, honored Ukrainian nationalists at a memorial in Babi Yar, where the most horrific massacre of Jews took place during the Holocaust. Not stopping there, Yushchenko bestowed the government's highest honor on none other than Stepan Bandera, a leader of the OUN.

Perhaps, Yushchenko's efforts helped rehabilitate Bandera and others in the minds of many. Indeed, rightists brandished a host of OUN and UPA flags on Maidan square while belting out partisan wartime songs. If anything, the UPA's popularity has soared ominously since Maidan. Even more disturbingly, a number of OUN-UPA apologists have been promoted to important government posts in Kiev, and Poroshenko has done nothing to confront the radical right. In fact, the President has gone out of his way to follow in the footsteps of reactionary predecessor Yushchenko by once again laying a wreath in honor of the OUN at Babi Yar. In addition, Poroshenko has referred to the UPA as "defenders of the fatherland" and established an official holiday in honor of the partisans. Needless to say, Putin and Russian media have made a lot of hay out of Kiev's backward politics and the emergence of so-called fascist hardliners.

Predictably, Kiev's new legislation has drawn international fire from a variety of quarters. The U.S. Holocaust Memorial Museum has protested the measures, noting "as Ukraine advances on the difficult road to full democracy, we strongly urge the nation's government to refrain from any measure that preempts or censors discussion or politicizes the study of history." The Organization for Security and Cooperation in Europe (OSCE) has echoed such sentiments, noting that "broadly and vaguely defined language that restricts individuals from expressing views on past events and people, could easily lead to suppression of political, provocative and critical speech, especially in the media."

Perhaps, the new legislation could even harm Ukraine's bid to join the European Union. Dolinsky writes "modern Ukrainians need to realize and comprehend this difficult and tragic history in order to become a truly European nation. Such laws as that recently signed by President Poroshenko can only harm the Ukrainian people." Others worry about the chilling effect which legislation could exert upon scholarship. Writing in the History News Network, academic experts declare that "the danger is that a prohibition on 'insulting' the 'fighters' or questioning the legitimacy of their 'struggle' is tantamount to a ban on critical research. The law does not specify what constitutes 'insulting', raising the question as to what scholars of modern Ukrainian history are allowed to write and say, and what they are not."

# CHAPTER 6

# Creating a New National Identity

CONTROVERSY SWIRLING AROUND THE HISTORIC role of OUN and UPA highlights Ukrainian soul searching and the quest for national identity. Though Ukraine has its right wing agitators and even mainstream apologists, the country has by and large practiced tolerance and inclusiveness since independence in 1991. Unfortunately, however, backward legislation may serve to obscure the record. According to the *Christian Science Monitor*, recent political firestorms demonstrate that "the debate over Ukrainian fascist history isn't simply a he-said-she-said between Moscow and Kiev, but a deeper problem of how to square Ukraine's sometimes sordid past with its efforts to find a modern identity."

While the recent World War II flak poses thorny questions for many in Ukraine proper, the *imbroglio* may prompt soul searching within the wider foreign Diaspora, too. In the New York metropolitan area, the Ukrainian community numbers more than 100,000 people. In Manhattan's East Village, sometimes known as "Little Ukraine," locals expressed opposition to Russian influence while holding fundraisers in support of Maidan protest. Though the East Village has become gentrified in recent years, the neighborhood still sports landmarks such as the Association of Ukrainian-Americans; the Ukrainian National Home; the Veselka restaurant; a Ukrainian Church, and the local Ukrainian Museum.

Uniting the Ukrainian-American community against external threats is one thing, but looking inward and trying to define the new soul of a nation is another. Perhaps, as Kiev's political class increasingly moves to coddle extremist constituencies, the foreign Ukrainian community will undertake serious reflection. Though World War II is long over, the conflict still lives on for many in Ukraine and abroad. While Moscow has sought to exploit the fact that some Ukrainians collaborated with Germany during World War II, Kiev bristles defensively. Desperate to attract foreign sympathy and support, Ukraine has sought to cast itself in the best possible historic light in relation to its own World War II record.

For the outside world, such debates might seem a little outlandish or even arcane. On the other hand, historical victimhood has become an essential ingredient in newfound Ukrainian identity. Currently, there are more than 20 million Ukrainians living abroad. One large expat community resides in the U.S. and numbers nearly 1 million. Canada meanwhile has a very sizable Ukrainian Diaspora community numbering 1.2 million people. Many Ukrainian-Canadians had parents or grandparents who left Ukraine as a result of Stalin-orchestrated famine during the 1930s or post-war Soviet crackdown on Ukrainian nationalism. As a result, such folk may view the current war as a mere extension of Ukraine's longstanding struggle to free itself from Moscow's orbit.

During the recent conflict with Russian-backed separatists, the Ukrainian Diaspora has played an important role in shoring up the Kiev government. Indeed, the expat community has provided humanitarian relief and even hosted displaced refugees in its own homes. Such positive developments aside, there's another political dimension to the Ukrainian Diaspora which is all too seldom explored. Recently, professor of foreign policy Olena Lennon moved from her native Ukraine and put down roots in the U.S. Writing in *Foreign Affairs*, she notes that some Diaspora Ukrainians are "preoccupied with historical victimization." Recent fighting in the Ukrainian east, she adds, has "reignited" such sentiment while fueling radical nationalism. Chiming in for good measure, two other academics note that "a significant section of the Ukrainian Diaspora abroad, have too often reflexively taken a right-or-wrong-our-freedom-fighters approach to wartime and postwar ethnic nationalists. Yet, at crucial points, these nationalists stood for forms of authoritarianism not much less aggressive than those of the totalitarianism behemoths." To be sure, not all Ukrainians in the wider Diaspora share objectionable points of view. Yet there's enough here to warrant cause for concern. One letter to the editor of *Kyiv Post* notes the Diaspora's "right wing sympathies, somehow rationalized by its anti-communist traditions." Further experts note that the Diaspora has historically provided considerable financial backing for rightwing nationalists in Ukraine linked to Stepan Bandera.

In the midst of conflict with rebels in the east, such thorny history has assumed larger than life importance. According to scholar Himka, Ukrainians have been adept at fostering so-called "victimization narratives." Certainly, Himka writes, Stalinist-induced famine of the 1930s or other episodes of Ukrainian victimization are important topics of historical research. On the other hand, Himka adds, "I object to instrumentalizing this memory with the aim of generating political and moral capital, particularly when it is linked to an exclusion from historical research and reflection of events in which Ukrainians figured as perpetrators not victims, and when 'our own' evil is kept invisible and the memory of the others' dead is not held sacred."

Himka notes that Ukrainians of the Diaspora latch on to the 1932-33 famine in Soviet Ukraine but "there persists a deafening silence about, as well as reluctance to confront, even well-documented war crimes, such as the mass murder of Poles in Volhynia by the Ukrainian Insurgent Army (UPA) and the cooperation of the Ukrainian auxiliary police in the execution of the Jews." The historian adds that the Ukrainian Diaspora frequently employs a "double standard" when it comes to discussing war crimes committed by Ukrainians as opposed to injustices perpetrated against Ukrainians. "Memoirs and eye-witness accounts," he writes, "...are considered untrustworthy evidence for the former, but trustworthy for the latter; that is, Jewish or Polish first-hand accounts of Ukrainian war crimes are dismissed as biased, while an important Ukrainian victimization narrative, the famine of 1932-33, has relied primarily on just such eyewitness accounts."

It is to be hoped that the right will not shape Ukrainian identity in the midst of war, though political pressures have brought retrograde forces into the public eye. *Foreign Affairs* writes, "Ukrainians are already bombarded by the propaganda of two extreme ideologies: one from right-wing Ukrainian nationalists and the other from the Kremlin. This fire doesn't need more fuel from the Diaspora." Himka, meanwhile, believes it is high time Ukrainians developed a more inclusive identity and collective memory. "There has to be a space created for those who want to maintain a relation to the Ukrainian identity but also want to move beyond a rhetoric of denial and victimization," he writes, "a rhetoric sounding increasingly shrill and hollow. We need a healthier collective memory firmly rooted in truthfulness."

Not stopping there, Himka has a word or two for the Diaspora. The expat community, he says, must "reach out to and communicate with the other. Only soul-searching can open the door to reconciliation and to the elaboration of an understanding of the past that can be shared by Ukrainians, Jews and Poles. Otherwise the situation will remain as it is today, with several competing hermetic narratives of what happened during the war. The Ukrainian Diaspora narrative, which had never been very convincing to outsiders, is becoming even less so. It is time to revise what we remember."

## MYTHOLOGIZING THE PAST

Just who has a monopoly on victimization? The Ukrainian Diaspora in Canada has adopted a defensive posture when it comes to the historical record. Rather perversely, the Ukrainian Canadian Civil Liberties Association opposed the creation of a Canadian museum devoted exclusively to the memory of the Holocaust. No funding should be allotted, organizers argued, unless the museum also agreed to showcase Soviet oppression of Ukraine and the Holodomor, or Stalinist-induced famine of 1932-33. In an effort to force Ukrainian peasants to join collective farms, Stalin commandeered farmers' grain and other foodstuffs. The result was disastrous as millions of Ukrainians starved and perished. In some regions, the death rate reached one third of the population with entire villages laid waste.

Hoping to bolster its case against Moscow, Ukraine as well as the country's foreign Diaspora have zeroed in on the Holodomor. Within the currently hyper-charged political *milieu*, the famine has become a source of great controversy. On the one hand, Ukrainians argue the famine constitutes genocide since the Holodomor targeted ethnic Ukrainians and was a direct result of Stalin's forced collectivization and massive grain exports. According to historians, the famine reflected Stalin's drive to stamp out Ukrainian nationalism which had earlier come to the fore during the country's civil war. Experts believe Stalin could have spared Ukraine if he had redirected grain exports to feed the peasants. On the other hand, the Kremlin claims the famine was not organized along strictly ethnic lines. In this version, the Holodomor was the simple result of a poor crop season and Soviet inability to harvest grain.

Eager to prosecute the public relations war, Poroshenko has compared the Holodomor to the conflict with Russian-backed separatists. Not surprisingly, Kiev observes the Holodomor every year on November 22, the official day of commemoration. Olga Bielkova, a member of the Ukrainian parliament, has made historical comparisons between Soviet famine and Putin's undeclared war. Writing in the Huffington Post, she remarks "a justification offered by Stalin at the time was the need for rapid industrialization at all cost, but what really bothered him about Ukraine was our unbending desire for self-determination."

The Kremlin, she adds, "is still denying [the] Holodomor. Many Russians influenced by the propaganda pedaled by the state-run TV stations genuinely

Memorial to the Holodomor in Kiev.

believe that Ukraine is not an independent state, that [the] breakup of the Soviet Union is a mistake and Putin is the one to correct it, that Ukrainian is not a language but rather a dialect of Russian and that dreams of Ukrainians therefore deserve no attention." Not surprisingly, pro-Russian rebels have struck back with their own version of historical events. Within the Donetsk People's Republic in the east, teachers have been forced to trash old textbooks and teach Ukrainian history in accordance with new guidelines stipulating that the Holodomor wasn't genocide but rather a "tragedy" which afflicted the entire Soviet Union.

## RECONSIDERING HISTORIC ROLE MODELS

As Ukraine sorts out its post-Maidan *milieu*, the country must wrestle with thorny political history. Who are the historic role models most worthy of praise and emulation? At this point it's too early to say who will win the contested battle over history. Unfortunately, however, Ukraine seems to have elevated more conservative and right wing historic figures while neglecting or even obliterating the memory of its own liberal and more radical leftist past.

Writing in the *New Republic*, Rutgers historian Jochen Hellbeck notes that new laws on historical memory condemn both Communist and Nazi regimes of the past, and ban propagandistic use of their symbols. However, the law mostly focuses on the Soviet era while ignoring atrocities committed against the Jews, "let alone the participation of Ukrainians in these atrocities." The legislation, which was shuttled through parliament without public discussion, outrageously threatens those holding alternative historical views with prison terms of up to ten years.

In the wake of Maidan, the country must sort out its identity and history.

Hellbeck writes that the omission of certain historic controversies is strategic, since another law actually glorifies partisans affiliated with the Ukrainian Insurgent Army or UPA, which collaborated with the German Wehrmacht. During World War II, the UPA emerged as a nationalist guerrilla outfit which battled Soviet, Polish, and Czech forces in the name of independence. However, at one stage during the conflict the UPA also cooperated with the Nazis. When Germans entered the western Ukrainian city of Lviv in June, 1941 Bandera's nationalists joined Nazi Einsatzgruppen in carrying out pogroms against the Jews.

In 1943, when the Germans fled Ukraine, many local policemen who had collaborated with the Nazis joined the UPA and committed atrocities against ethnic minorities. By war's end, it was said that both organizations which had been led by Bandera, that is to say the UPA as well as the Organization of Ukrainian Nationalists (OUN), engaged in atrocities against Poles, Jews and others.

In light of such history, one might think the UPA would be reviled in the court of public opinion. However, spectators cheered UPA veterans at one VE-Day celebration in Kiev. Poroshenko himself presided over the event, though the president failed to mention the plight of Ukrainian Jews in his speech. In another alarming case, protesters clashed with police outside parliament when legislators failed to support a bill recognizing the UPA. The bill would have restored "historical justice" and paid respect to the outfit. Reportedly, between 8,000-10,000 people showed up for the Kiev protest, which at one point turned violent as militants threw smoke and flash-bang devices at the authorities. Somewhat ominously, Ukrainian television showed protesters brandishing banners of right wing Svoboda Party, which seeks historical recognition for the UPA. In the midst of war against Russian separatists in the east, some members of Svoboda have embraced Bandera, who was eventually killed by the KGB, as a nationalist figure.

## COMING TO TERMS WITH HISTORY

To this day, Ukraine continues to wrestle with its wartime past. In Kiev's Museum of the Great Patriotic War, visitors are greeted with displays of Soviet military insignias and medals awarded to courageous fighters who battled Nazi Germany. How does one square such history with the decidedly mixed legacy of Bandera? To be sure, Bandera collaborated with the Nazis though he was also imprisoned subsequently in a German concentration camp. Ukrainian nationalist goals, in fact, were not identical to the Third Reich's. While Bandera's followers were responsible for murdering Jews, their ideology wasn't entirely anti-Semitic but rather pro-Ukrainian. That is to say, they wanted their opponents out of the way and saw many local Jews as pro-Soviet.

Some Bandera veterans survive even to this day, which makes coming to terms with history doubly confounding.

Outside Museum of the Great Patriotic War in Kiev. Recently, Ukraine's World War II record has surfaced as a hot button political issue.

Shekhovtsov, the expert on the European far right, says history textbooks from central or western Ukraine don't mention that members of Bandera's movement were involved in the Holocaust and pogroms in Lviv. Rather, he adds, Bandera is blandly described as a national liberation fighter. On the other hand, Shekhovtsov explained to me, "Bandera has been glorified not because he was an anti-Semite but because he was a nationalist figure who fought against Soviet influence. When people glorify him, it doesn't mean they are aware of this dark history or even endorse anti Semitism."

Back in the old Jewish quarter of Podil, Zissels says the majority of the UPA refrained from taking part in anti-Jewish executions. Mostly, he added, it was the Germans who committed atrocities along with local police units comprised of many different ethnic groups including Ukrainians, Belarussians, Russians and even some Muslims. "There's almost no connection between Bandera and present day Ukraine," Zissels remarked matter-of-factly.

Pilash, on the other hand, is more concerned about Bandera's historical legacy and links to present day politics. To be sure, he concedes, Bandera served time in a concentration camp and did not coordinate wartime atrocities directly. However, Pilash added, when nationalists highlight the fact that Bandera was imprisoned, this serves to obscure inconvenient truths. Whether he was a fascist, an "integral nationalist," or "proto-fascist," Bandera was a far right totalitarian figure opposed to sharing political power with Poles, Russians and Jews.

Denis Pilash

It is dispiriting, Pilash explained, that many young Ukrainians still look upon Bandera as a national hero. In general, he said, there's a consensus in wider society that Ukrainian nationalism has always been emancipating. What you wind up with, he added, is a "very ethno-centric view" of the past which doesn't help to promote the notion of a truly multi-ethnic society. "Many people," he remarked, "including liberals, whitewash the history of the OUN. If you say Bandera is a fascist today, people think you are some kind of Moscow propagandist."

## COSSACK REVIVAL

In Ukrainian consciousness, the notion of the "Cossack" looms large, and during protests against Yanukovych and subsequent drive to war with Russian separatists, many fell back on somewhat questionable historical

At Kiev's Museum of the Great Patriotic War, Ukrainian sacrifice is extolled though some have failed to come to terms with other darker chapters of the conflict.

associations. Indeed, traditional symbolism was very much apparent at Kiev's Maidan Square, with some nationalist protesters even sporting Cossack-style costumes and hairstyles. Instilled with a sense of pride, the National Art Museum stocks display cases full of ethnic artifacts such as Cossack musical instruments. Those Ukrainians who read are surely aware of dark Cossack history, though many others may simply view Cossacks as colorful and merry folk from the countryside.

Back in Kiev, Zissels took a somewhat more nuanced view. To be sure, he declares, Cossacks took part in anti-Jewish pogroms. On the other hand, French crusaders committed all types of abuses, but that does not necessarily imply that contemporary French society has a medieval outlook. Just what are we to make of the new Cossack mythology? Certainly, modern self-styled Cossacks are more likely to collect folk music than to be carrying out pogroms. Displays of traditional Ukrainian folklore and clothing have proliferated meanwhile, all of which seem rather harmless. According to researcher Bezruk, local businesses selling such wares are more visible since Maidan protests and the eruption of war against Russian separatists in the east.

Meanwhile, though some have championed retrograde historical figures, a few bright spots give reason for hope. Taras Shevchenko, a prominent nineteenth century poet, has become an icon and symbol of national pride. For many, Shevchenko carries just as much stature as Shakespeare in England. Shevchenko's poems are inextricably linked to his own harsh life: born a serf, he was later freed from bondage. Politically, Shevchenko advocated the abolition of serfdom as well as Ukrainian independence. Shevchenko's poems, which were written in Ukrainian, criticized Russian oppression and drew the attention of Czarist authorities. As a result, Shevchenko was arrested and banished to an army post.

Because he was a fervent critic of Moscow, Shevchenko is a convenient historic role model for patriotic Ukrainians. During anti-Yanukovych demonstrations, protesters carved a wooden sculpture of the poet near Maidan square. The structure is one of many thousands of Shevchenko statues spread out all over Ukraine. After Yanukovych's fall, the new government in Kiev hailed Shevchenko as an inspiration to the Maidan movement. In March, 2014 Ukrainians celebrated the bicentennial of

In an underground passage beneath Maidan square, a local store displays traditional Ukrainian clothing.

Traditional Ukrainian woman.

In the wake of revolt against Yanukovych, Ukrainians have
celebrated historic icons such as Shevchenko, whose image has
been commercialized in kitschy shops around Maidan.

Shevchenko's birth. In Kiev, Maidan activists laid wreaths at his statue
while others plastered the city with celebratory posters. In Crimea, however, the commemoration was met with political strife as pro-Russian activists attacked Ukrainians near a local Shevchenko monument.

Off Maidan square, a politicized portrait of noted nineteenth century poet Taras Shevchenko who advocated for the abolition of serfdom as well as Ukrainian independence.

A politicized Maidan portrait of noted nineteenth century poet Taras Shevchenko. The caption underneath reads, "Fire doesn't burn those who are fierce."

# Obliterating Ukraine's Revolutionary Past

Instead of harking back to questionable historic role models, Ukrainians might want to reconsider the country's idealistic and progressive heritage. Specifically, Ukrainians might take a second look at Nestor Makhno, an anarchist revolutionary who fought against the forces of reaction during the civil war. Born into the peasantry, Makhno later became a kind of Robin Hood-style bandit, stealing from the rich and giving to the poor. Arrested by Czarist authorities, Makhno became a voracious reader in jail and received the political education which had earlier eluded him. Amidst revolution in 1917, the peasant revolutionary was freed and amazingly the bandit managed to consolidate a free state in southeastern Ukraine.

Hoping to liberate the peasantry and cultivate a system of self-governing communes, Makhno audaciously took on not only Bolsheviks but also the conservative White army, occupying German and Austrian forces and even the authorities in Kiev. Unlike the Ukrainian government, Makhno adopted a strong stand against anti-Semitism and some claim that anarchist forces displayed a much better record than rival armies in this regard. Fighting under their characteristic black banner, Makhno's guerrilla forces launched covert raids, distributed goods to the peasants and managed to gain the trust of the local population. Eventually, however, Makhno was overwhelmed by the Bolsheviks and was forced into exile, having failed to secure his dream of a truly independent anarchist Ukraine. Of all the historical figures swirling around the Ukrainian civil war, Makhno is arguably the most worthy of praise. Yet oddly, Makhno's legacy has been obscured and marginalized. To be sure, activist Pilash told me, Makhno is occasionally highlighted in popular culture and the revolutionary remains a great symbol of freedom against authority. In this sense, Makhno reinforces tough and sturdy myths about the Ukrainian character.

In 2014, Makhno's home town celebrated the revolutionary's 125th birthday, though the event was reportedly a "relatively muted affair" and there was no nation-wide remembrance. Speaking with *New Left Review*, sociologist

Volodymyr Ishchenko remarks, "the right has worked to reinterpret figures such as Makhno along nationalist lines—not as an anarchist, but as another Ukrainian who fought against communism. In their eyes communism was a Russian imposition, and anarchism too is depicted as 'anti-Ukrainian'" Pilash agrees, adding that Ukraine's leftist history has been largely forgotten and therefore he and his colleagues must "rescue" figures like Makhno amidst Ukraine's contentious and ongoing debates over the course of its political past and future.

## Nationalist Flags, Insignia and Curious Symbolism

During protests against Yanukovych, Kiev's Maidan square was full of activist encampments and a plethora of diverse political flags. On the Maidan, nationalism was often associated with pro-European Union sentiment, and E.U. blue and yellow flags could be seen fluttering alongside the Ukrainian flag. In the wake of demonstrations which toppled the regime, such outward displays are somewhat less evident on the square, which can seem rather empty during weekdays. Indeed, during the first few days of my stay I didn't see overt political symbolism on Maidan though one young woman brandished her own home-made blue flag reading "tours."

Nevertheless, impromptu rallies on weekends may elicit occasional interest of passers-by. At one point, I came upon a group of nationalists in Maidan square flanked by Ukrainian blue and yellow banners and a rather sinister-looking bunch of men in sunglasses. The demonstrators sought to subject officials and politicians to so-called "lustration." After the fall of the Soviet Union, the term lustration was used to describe the purge of Communist *apparatchnicks*, though it has also been applied to former members of the Yanukovych government.

Look closely on the weekend, and further displays of political symbolism are apparent. Off Maidan square, I come upon a group of people brandishing flags. At first I thought the banners might be communist, since the flags were red. However, banners displayed no iconic hammer and sickle but instead fluttered

A politicized portrait of Ivan Franko, a noted nineteenth century author, who wears an iconic construction helmet which was common on the Maidan. Franko was an author, journalist and political activist who advocated socialism and Ukrainian nationalism.

Woman waves a blue tour flag in Maidan square.

the numbers "5.10." Later, while carrying out interviews around Kiev, I inquired about the flags and their meaning. Activist Pilash explained that the red flag bearers hail from something called the "5.10" party. "These people are extremely libertarian and fundamentalist about the free market," Pilash said. "They wish to completely deregulate the economy and cut social expenditures to 'stimulate investment,'" he added. Genady Belashov, leader of the 5.10 party, favors the elimination of all taxes except for two, a 5% sales tax and a 10% social tax. Not surprisingly, right wing *Forbes* magazine finds the 5.10 party "interesting." If they took a tour of Kiev and happened upon a statue of a red bull emblazoned with the numbers 5.10, Wall Street tycoons would probably feel right at home.

A rally on Maidan square pushing for "lustration" and getting rid
of elements associated with the old Yanukovych regime.

## CONTOURS OF UKRAINIAN NATIONALISM

It's a little ironic that such right wing economics would find a receptive audience
near Maidan square, with its austere looking Soviet realist architecture. Yet in the
wake of the Soviet Union's collapse, newfound political movements have rushed
to fill the ideological vacuum. In the midst of war with Russian separatists in the
east, patriotic symbolism has become ever more prominent. To be sure, Maidan is
less politicized than before, though I saw many Kiev buildings outside the square
which were draped with national blue and yellow flags.

Bezruk, the researcher at the Congress of National Communities of
Ukraine, worries about the political mood in her country. "There are flags ev-
erywhere," she said, "and I am concerned about anti-Communist sentiment,
which is in reality anti-left. Nationalism is so strong now that sometimes it
makes me nervous." Indeed, many on the right wing circuit have failed to
distinguish between the old communist guard and Kiev's newly independent
left, which is labeled as Russian and anti-Ukrainian. So who owns Ukrainian
nationalist symbolism? In and around Maidan Square, I saw mementoes to

Elderly men take in the lustration rally.

Patriotism on display near Maidan square.

fallen martyrs who had been killed whilst participating in anti-Yanukovych protest. Wrapped around a tree, one memento was dotted with blue and yellow ribbon and dedicated to a fallen hero. In a photo, a man poses at a political event featuring right wing nationalist party Svoboda.

During unrest at Maidan square, Svoboda comprised much of the "street muscle," with club wielding activists sporting bicycle helmets as well as ski masks. Party members brandished the old UPA flag which is black and red, colors which stand for blood and soil. Svoboda claims that history has misjudged the UPA's record and therefore Ukraine should honor partisan fighters' memory in sports stadiums. Controversially, party members honor veterans of the Waffen SS's local Halychyna brigade, a unit constituted in 1943 to fight the Soviets.

Anarchists, on the other hand, fall back upon Makhno's black flag which sports skull and crossbones and a motto below reading "Death to all who stand in the way of freedom for working people!" During protests at Maidan square, activist Neshevets and her colleagues campaigned for progressive reform including free transportation and education. It wasn't long, however, before rightist street thugs attacked the left, grabbing anarchist flags and crushing them. "Before Maidan," she says, "I wasn't so attuned to nationalism. But then I started to attend demonstrations and what the hell? Some guys are attacking me and shouting something against the Jews. I was really shocked: for the first time I was face to face with Nazis and they were real and trying to beat me up as well as my friends."

A woman wears national blue and yellow colors at the theater near Maidan square.

Memento to a fallen Svoboda martyr killed during the EuroMaidan revolution.

# CHAPTER 7

# Plight of Ethnic Minorities

AMIDST ALL THE MEDIA FRENZY surrounding Putin's nefarious destabilization efforts in Eastern Ukraine, other issues of vital importance have gone ignored. Take, for example, the plight of ethnic Tatars, a group which is predominantly Sunni Muslim and traces its roots back to Turkic and Mongol tribes. Tatar men are distinguished by their distinctive hats and women by their headscarves. There are currently millions of Tatars spread throughout eastern Russia and Ukraine. Some also live in the contentious Crimean peninsula, where they represent some 15 percent of the local population.

Reportedly, Ukrainians and Tatars enjoyed a degree of peaceful co-existence after Kiev achieved independence from the Soviet Union in 1991. In fact, researcher Bezruk says Ukraine was tolerant of local mosques. According to the *New Republic*, Tatars even supported the Kiev government when Ukrainian politicians held up land restitution claims and calls for greater autonomy. Indeed, Ukrainian rule failed to encourage efforts at cultural self-expression and in 2009, Bezruk remarks, "I was doing some research about Tatar efforts to preserve their language. At that time, we only found pre-schools where Crimean Tatar was being taught and spoken. The children learned some songs and poems, but they did not use their language in everyday life, choosing instead to speak Russian."

Whatever the historic problems, it is probably fair to say that Tatars, who suffered under Czarist and later Soviet rule, enjoyed much better historic relations with Ukraine than Russia. Not surprisingly, therefore, Putin's annexation of Crimea, which wrested control over the peninsula from Kiev, has brought back uncomfortable memories for Tatars. The latter in fact largely boycotted Putin's referendum which resulted in outright Russian annexation of Crimea. Later, the *mejlis* or main Tatar governing body refused to recognize official Russian rule. Nevertheless, the *Guardian* of London notes that "many Crimean Tatars have decided that, unwilling to leave their homeland, it is better to find a *modus vivendi* with Russia rather than be in permanent opposition." Hoping to sway the local population against Kiev, Putin has reportedly invested in housing and support for Crimean Tatars.

Ukrainian authorities, meanwhile, haven't made a very persuasive case to the Tatars. So says Myroslav Marynovych, Vice-Rector of the Ukrainian Catholic University in Lviv, who wrote a critical column about Kiev's handling of the Crimea situation. Even when Tatars called out for help, he notes, Ukraine proved to be tone deaf and pulled its forces out of Crimea, thus "leaving the Tatars to fend for themselves." Sounding a sober note, Marynovych notes "the Crimean Tatars now have no good options." Tatars who opt to stay in Crimea must abide by the terms of Russian rule, that is to say they must accept Russian passports. But new measures place Tatars in a bind, since anyone filing for Russian citizenship must give up their Ukrainian passports. Russian law, in fact, has criminalized undeclared dual citizenship and imposes fines on those who fail to inform authorities of having obtained such citizenship in another country. In effect, however, the new measures are a moot point for Crimean Tatars, since Kiev prohibits dual citizenship anyway.

Refat Chubarov, a Tatar leader, feels caught in a strange catch-22. Speaking to the media, he remarked "People may be forced to become citizens of the country that forced this situation on them, as well as being citizens of the country that was unable to defend them." Perhaps, Marynovych laments, "Ukraine could have made an exception to its ban on dual citizenship for Tatars, which would have made the practicalities of life much easier and would have signified that the Ukrainian state is sensitive toward them." Unfortunately, however, Kiev has not been proactive, and though the Ukrainian parliament recently recognized Tatars as the native people of Crimea, such "recognition came much too late, causing nothing but frustration and disappointment."

# Tatars and World War II

Moscow's annexation of Crimea brings back uncomfortable historic memories for local Tatars. Specifically, Josef Stalin's fateful 1944 decision to deport all 200,000 Crimean Tatars to the east still carries unpleasant associations. Stalin justified his horrific decision by claiming the Tatars had collaborated with the Nazis. About half the Crimean Tatar population died during or as a result of deportations, and those who managed to survive were deprived of their possessions. Tatars were only allowed to return to Crimea in 1988, at which point many sought to reclaim their ancestral lands.

Within the current politically-charged *milieu*, the debate surrounding Tatars and their historic role exerts renewed importance. Writing in the *Encyclopedia of the World's Minorities*, Carl Skutsch notes that "Tatar collaboration with the German regime is one of the most controversial topics in Soviet history." Initially, he says, Tatars viewed the Nazi invasion as a "sign of hope." For years, Tatars had been subjected to persecution under both Czarist and Soviet authorities and erroneously believed the Germans might help to ameliorate their plight. It's all rather disappointing to be sure, though Skutsch adds that "the extent of the Tatars' anti-Soviet behavior is a topic of ongoing dispute."

In seeking to justify its clampdown, Moscow charged that the Tatars had fought against Soviet partisans; participated in German self-defense battalions, and provided intelligence to the Nazis. The total number of Tatars who assisted the Germans was 20,000 or ten percent of the population at the time. On the other hand, Skutsch adds that "Crimean Tatar participation was not necessarily voluntary, often being secured at gunpoint." Independent scholar Otto Pohl notes that German military authorities in Crimea rounded up Tatar P.O.W.'s in January 1942 and formed the latter into self-defense battalions. The Tatars volunteered on the condition they would be released from prison camps and given better rations.

It seems a little debatable whether the Tatars actually "collaborated" with the Nazis or were coerced into servitude in the face of starvation or even death. Moreover, Russian apologists who impugn Tatars today are falling into an earlier tradition of Soviet scholarship which sought to blacken the Tatars' reputation. Historians in fact ignored the fact that perhaps 50,000 or more Tatars fought in the Red Army against the Nazis. Such Tatar contributions are all the more remarkable when one considers that Soviet partisan units led by Russians and Ukrainians led a scorched earth policy against Tatar villages and civilians. Pohl notes that "this activity frequently had more to do with Slavic animosity towards the Crimean Tatars than any real [Nazi] collaboration by the victimized villagers."

In light of such history, should we dismiss accusations against the Tatars? Perhaps not entirely: Yitzhak Arad has carried out disturbing research suggesting that some Tatars weren't completely innocent during the occupation. In his book *The Holocaust in the Soviet Union,* Arad notes the Nazis eliminated the entire Crimean Jewish community between November, 1941 and March, 1942. "In cooperation with the village heads and the active participation of local police forces," Arad writes, "the Einsatzgruppen did not miss a single rural settlement, even those with a minute Jewish community." Arad adds that "other groups involved in the murder of Jews in the Crimea consisted of companies of Tatar volunteers. In January 1942 a company of Tatar volunteers was established in Simferopol under the command of Einsatzgruppe 11. This company participated in anti-Jewish manhunts and murder actions in the rural regions."

Though certainly horrible, such atrocities don't imply that all Tatars were somehow guilty, let alone justify mass deportations. Pohl remarks that self-defense units "became the basis behind the slanderous charge by the Stalin regime that the entire Crimean Tatar nation actively collaborated with Nazi Germany against the Soviet Union. Despite an official recognition of the falsehood of this charge by the Soviet government in 1967, it is still repeated by some Russian chauvinists today."

## DELICATE STATUS

From Soviet deportation to Putin's recent annexation of Crimea, the Tatars have always been forced to navigate a fraught political path. Under Ukrainian rule, Tatars achieved some modest success. After some Tatars returned from forced Stalinist deportation, they immediately embarked on a building spree. Under Ukrainian rule, Tatars became educated and the young traveled to Turkey where they obtained university degrees. Later, Tatars entered the business world and some achieved success while working in large cities like Kiev.

Despite these advances, however, most Tatars wound up laboring in agriculture, construction and the service sector. Moreover, in the midst of repatriation efforts, Tatars encountered discrimination within wider society. From 2007 to 2011, while she was studying in Crimea, Bezruk observed the material conditions facing Tatars. "I lived in a dormitory," she remarks. "I lived on the third floor, but on the first floor you had Tatars who had returned from earlier deportation." Bezruk says those Tatars who she came across had jobs, though their material circumstances left something to be desired. "The families and children had nowhere to go," Bezruk reports, "and so they had to live in the dormitory. It was painful to see grandmothers having to cook in the student kitchen."

Whatever the case, it seems clear that if forced to choose between outright Russian annexation or discrimination and mixed job prospects under Kiev, most Tatars would choose the latter. According to Bezruk, Tatars consistently voted against Yanukovych, a politician who failed to encourage local autonomy and sought to move his country into Moscow's orbit. When protests erupted in Kiev against Yanukovych, Tatars moved to support the burgeoning EuroMaidan movement and some even participated in demonstrations. At Maidan Square, protesters brandished blue and yellow Ukrainian flags, European Union flags, blue Crimean Tatar flags, and even a curious hybrid E.U.-Crimean Tatar flag. Meanwhile, an improvised Tatar band played music onstage.

In Crimea itself, Maidan protests took on a distinctly anti-Russian character amidst signs that Moscow might annex the peninsula. The Russian majority in Crimea is comprised of people who moved to the area after World War II, and reportedly they strongly identify with Soviet and earlier Czarist imperial narratives. Not surprisingly, then, local protests pitted pro-Maidan Tatars against pro-Kremlin supporters who denounced Kiev demonstrators as "bandits." Nervously, Tatars brandished their own pale blue flag while shouting "Ukraine! Ukraine!" while Russians, some of them Cossacks dressed in traditional clothing, retorted "Crimea is Russian!" Anti-Maidan Russians later blasted religious songs on amplifiers set up at a local church (ironically enough, Ukrainians are also fond of their own Cossack tradition and some EuroMaidan protesters held ties to the Orthodox Church). Later, some Tatars who chose not to boycott the referendum vote were turned away at the polls while their ID cards were confiscated.

For those Tatars who chose to stay in Crimea after Russian annexation, life remains a daily challenge. In the wake of the referendum which led Crimea to separate from Ukraine, local authorities asked Tatars to vacate their land. Since then, Tatars complain their homes have been marked with ominous crosses on doors. Meanwhile, a Tatar activist went missing and another was found murdered in a local forest. Prior to his disappearance, the activist was seen in the clutches of menacing Russian militias. Fearful of full-scale style ethnic cleansing, some Tatar men are reportedly relocating their families abroad. Marynovych of the Ukrainian Catholic University notes, "They [Tatars] supported us on the Maidan, and we abandoned them to the mercy of the Russian occupiers. The loss of their trust in Ukraine is a psychological wound that will take a long time to heal."

To its credit, the western Ukrainian city of Lviv has hosted such refugees, though reportedly some are unhappy with the newcomers. Bezruk, who monitors hate crimes throughout Ukraine, tells me that Tatars arrived in Lviv without any jobs. Mostly, she adds, the migrants speak Russian, which marks them as outsiders in a city known for its Ukrainian nationalism. Bezruk adds that Muslim women migrants sporting headscarves have been attacked in Lviv, though the assailants remain unidentified.

## OTHER MINORITIES

Historically, Jews of Crimea look back on their long past in utopian terms. Some survivors may in fact recall nominally autonomous Soviet-era Jewish districts with fondness. At the time, Yiddish language schools were common in Crimea and students studied math, history, Marxism-Leninism and farming techniques. Classes were held in Yiddish, and residents enjoyed performances at local Crimean Yiddish state theaters. Such utopian history, however, has been obscured by political developments in Ukraine. Amidst the contentious political standoff between Kiev and Moscow, Crimean Jews have been forced to choose sides.

According to *Kyiv Post*, Crimea's 12,000 Jews have been split over Russian annexation of their region, and some have supported the Kremlin in opposition to their peers back in Kiev. To be sure, Russian pledges of higher pensions helped to secure Jewish support. Furthermore, the main language on the peninsula has always been Russian, and when Putin annexed the Crimea he sought to justify his actions by promising to protect the rights of not only Russian speakers but also other ethnic minorities including Jews. For some in the local Jewish community, such pledges were welcome. Meanwhile, though some media reports exaggerated anti-Semitic elements at the Maidan, such accounts were apparently enough to sway some of Crimea's Jews to the Russian side.

Tatars aren't the only ones who have been forced to navigate a delicate line. In Crimea, two small minority groups, the Karaites and Krymchaks, have been caught in the political crosshairs. Crimean Karaites, a Turkic-speaking ethnic group, have backed Russia's annexation of Crimea, while the Krymchaks, a similarly Turkic group, have preferred to stay neutral. While it might seem a little surprising that such groups have supported the Kremlin, or at least chosen to remain silent, such developments are somewhat understandable in light of tumultuous history.

Take a stroll through downtown Kiev today and the vestiges of Karaite culture are still visible. Walking along Yaroslaviv Val Street, I spot an impressive architectural masterpiece called a "Kenasa," a Karaite term for synagogue. Typically, a Kenasa is a two-storey building with one floor reserved for men and the other for women. The faithful can only enter the Kenasa after washing both hands and faces and removing shoes. Originally built between 1898 and 1902 in Moorish style, the local Kiev Kenasa was constructed by Vladislav Gorodetsky, a famous architect of the day. During Soviet times, the temple served as a theater and was later converted into the Ukrainian House of Actors. In 1991 Ukraine achieved independence, though unfortunately the synagogue was never given back to the Karaite community.

Karaite kenasa in Kiev.

The Karaites have vanished from Kiev but an 800-strong flock continues to live on in Crimea, where adherents still boast two Kenasas. Though Karaites still adhere to the Torah, and keep a religious calendar which includes Rosh Hashanah, Passover and Shavuot, they don't define themselves as Jews. Though somewhat odd, such developments may have helped the Karaites preserve their culture in the long-term. Indeed, during the 19th century Karaites convinced anti-Talmud Czarist authorities that they should be treated differently from other Jews.

Despite such good fortune, the Karaites fell on hard times after the 1917 revolution. Once ensconced in power the Soviets persecuted the community, and in the city of Simferopol authorities replaced a Star of David atop the local Kenasa with a communist red star. Since 1936, the building has housed a radio broadcasting office, and today the local flock is obliged to pray in a local school building due to lack of a proper Kenasa. In total, only two Kenasas remain in Crimea, one in Yevpatoria and another within an ancient cave fortress located near the city of Bakhchysaray. Meanwhile, only about a dozen people still manage to speak Karaim fluently.

So where does the Karaite community stand in relation to other Jews in Crimea? A few years ago, Bezruk remarked, "We spoke with the Karaites and they said they weren't so comfortable in Crimea. They declared that the Ukrainian government had not recognized their culture." News reports tend to confirm such accounts. Indeed, Karaites have long sought to reclaim control over a local cemetery, Kenasas and the cave fortress near Bakhchysaray, though leaders say they ultimately failed to secure desired support from Ukrainian authorities. Such acrimonious disputes have led the Karaites to support Putin, as the community hopes the Russian leader will help to preserve the group's ancient culture. The majority of Karaites, in fact, reportedly voted for annexation. Karaites also backed Russia out of concern that lawlessness associated with EuroMaidan protests back in Kiev could spiral into instability.

Another Crimean minority group, the Krymchaks, has not fared as well as the Karaites. "Of Crimea's 120 nationalities," remarks *Kyiv Post*, "the Krymchaks have one of the longest histories on the peninsula, and one of the most tragic." Numbering only about 200 people, Krymchak Jews were devastated by World War II. In fact, thousands were wiped out during the Nazi occupation of Crimea and this has made the community quite guarded in its affairs.

"Caught between stronger, related cultural and ethnic groups in Crimea – Jewish, Russian, Crimean Tatar – which have offered help but threatened assimilation," notes *Kyiv Post*, "the few remaining Krymchaks have worked hard to preserve their history and identity." Today, the community maintains a small ethnographic museum in the city of Simferopol, where traditional scarves, dresses, belongings and photographs are held on public display.

In the wake of Putin's annexation, Krymchaks chose to stay neutral. Apparently, the local community's greatest priority wasn't securing language rights or higher pensions for that matter, but simply preserving the Krymchak museum for posterity. Brutalized and mistreated at different times in their history, Crimea's Karaites and Krymchaks are indeed survivors. Seen from afar, their choice to side with Putin or remain neutral may seem a little perverse, but in light of past history can one really blame either community for seeking to avoid conflict?

## RUSYNS AND ANDY WARHOL

As the Ukrainian crisis worsens, and the central government is revealed as incompetent and ineffectual, outside powers are stirring up mischief within the country's restive regions. Take, for example, Transcarpathia, which is known in Ukraine as Zakarpatts'ka Oblast,' though the region has displayed a bewildering array of other names throughout history. For the most part, ethnic minorities of Transcarpathia have gotten along with each other in recent years, though the area's delicate social balance could be upset by outsiders like Putin and his nationalist right wing allies in neighboring Hungary.

Transcarpathia is a multi-ethnic area lying on Ukraine's western border with Poland, Slovakia, Hungary and Romania. Though most of Transcarpathia, which takes its name from the Carpathian Mountain chain, lies within

Ukrainian borders, some of the region falls within boundaries of other neighboring countries. As Ukraine falters, poverty-stricken Transcarpathia may be a tempting target for outside opportunistic agitators. Though the region is only about 250 miles long by 60 miles wide, Transcarpathia is home to 1.2 million people and encompasses not only Russians and Ukrainians but also a variety of other ethnic groups.

Take, for example, the Rusyns or Ruthenians, an eastern Slavic people. The Rusyns comprise their own distinct ethno-linguistic group, and generally espouse a branch of Eastern Catholicism (perhaps the most famous individual of Ruthenian heritage is none other than Andy Warhol or Andrij Warhola, whose parents spoke native Rusyn). Traditionally, Rusyns lived in small, rural villages though in recent times they have migrated to larger cities such as Uzhhorod and Mukachevo. According to the World Academy of Carpatho-Rusyn Culture, seventy percent of the population still works in agriculture. Unfortunately, due to shortages of arable land, men are obliged to seek seasonal work and unemployment runs high.

Today, the Rusyns are doing their utmost to preserve their customs and traditions. In villages and larger towns such as Mukachevo, Rusyns have their own schools where children are instructed in local history, culture and language. However, the Ukrainian Ministry of Education has failed to fund the schools, which receive most of their support from Rusyn immigrants in North America. Moreover, Rusyns have recently grown alarmed by Ukrainian nationalists who employ xenophobic rhetoric against the community. Such trends are hardly a novel development: during Soviet times the authorities even banned the term "Rusyn" while the word "Ukrainian" was applied to all Rusyns living in Transcarpathia.

Michael Blain, a World War II survivor from Transcarpathia, wrote about such painful history in *Cleveland Jewish News*. In his piece, titled "My Country, Carpathia, Was Stolen," he writes that the Kremlin took over lands which did not belong to the Soviet Union. Prior to the war, Blain writes, Transcarpathia was in fact part of Czechoslovakia. In 1945, Blain looked for lost relatives in his Carpathian village, but found his homeland no longer formed part of Czechoslovakia. Instead, Soviet troops eventually annexed the area and incorporated Transcarpathia into the Ukrainian Soviet Republic. Blain writes ruefully, "Natives were told they weren't really Rusyns but Ukrainians, and it was said that the Rusyns asked to be incorporated into Ukraine. I saw no evidence of this."

## Transcarpathia Hungarians

To make matters even more complicated, Transcarpathia is also home to 162,000 Hungarians, the region's largest minority group. Reportedly, the Hungarians are Ukraine's "least assimilated" ethnic group. A full three quarters of them live within 30 miles of the Hungarian border, and nearly all hold their mother tongue. Like the Rusyns, Transcarpathia Hungarians are reportedly feeling nervous as Ukraine's far right groups become politically visible.

Take, for example, Pravy Sektor or "Right Sektor," a paramilitary outfit which stormed government buildings in the Carpathian towns of Berehove and Uzhhorod. Reportedly, the group was able to carry out its actions in the wake of Maidan protests and lack of central government control. Pravy Sektor militants claim they're not anti-Hungarian or anti-minority, though sensitive ethnic politics could exacerbate tensions. According to activist Pilash, who hails from Transcarpathia, the Ukrainian right has destroyed some shrines and monuments which were erected more than a thousand years ago when Hungarians migrated into the region. Fortunately, he adds, "there's been very little support in Transcarpathia for such actions."

Like many Russians in Crimea and eastern Ukraine, the Hungarians of Transcarpathia voted strongly for Yanukovych in the 2010 election, believing the candidate would be supportive of minority rights. Pravy Sektor, on the other hand, opposed Yanukovych during the Maidan protests and perceived the Ukrainian president as too beholden to outside Russian interests. Reportedly, some Ukrainians see the Hungarians as being "anti-Maidan," and in Uzhhorod a member of Pravy Sektor told the press that while he had nothing against Hungarians, "we have to fight the Russians."

Recent developments in Berehove and Uzhgorod are somewhat troubling. According to the American-Hungarian Federation, Ukrainian nationalists have "shown a penchant" for vandalizing Hungarian monuments in Transcarpathia and photos posted on the group's web site lend credence to such accounts. Additionally, the American-Hungarian Federation reports that "hate speech describing Hungarians as enemies of the Ukrainian people" surfaces on a regular basis. Hoping to counteract growing intolerance, the group hopes to foster a democratic and tolerant Ukraine, as opposed to a weak and corrupt country which "would enable Russia to fish in muddy waters." Above all, the outfit is concerned that "pro-Western" Hungarians might find themselves "inadvertent participants in the middle of a growing ethnic and East-West conflict."

In Transcarpathia, history is a potent reminder of long-held ethnic and cultural fissures. For 1,000 years, the area formed an integral part of Hungary and later the Austro-Hungarian Empire. After World War I and the fall of the Habsburgs in Vienna, Hungary was dismembered by the Entente powers. Under the 1920 Treaty of Trianon, ethnic Hungarian speakers in Transcarpathia were separated from their kinsmen in Budapest, and then the region was annexed by newly created Czechoslovakia for good measure. Needless to say, Hungarians living in Transcarpathia had little say in such matters as the allies ignored the principle of self-determination and a plebiscite was denied.

Not surprisingly, some on the Budapest far right scene have sought to capitalize on such history. Gábor Vona, who heads up far right Jobbik ("Movement for a Better Hungary"), the country's third largest party, has stated "What happened in the Trianon Palace in Versailles after the First World War was that the enemies of Hungary dictated the fate of our country on the basis of lies, manipulated figures, and false reports." Hostility toward minorities is all too common in Ukraine, Vona adds, and Kiev seeks to "forcefully assimilate" the Hungarians. On the party's website, Jobbik posts incendiary articles with titles such as "Hungarians under threat in the Lower Carpathians." Kiev authorities are "illegitimate," Jobbik claims, and fail to protect the country's ethnic minorities. Somewhat ominously, Jobbik held a protest in 2014 outside the Hungarian Foreign Ministry in Budapest with participants holding signs reading "Hungary wants Transcarpathia back!" Jobbik MP Tamás Gaudi-Nagy said the goal of the protest was to "support the sovereignty demands of our Hungarian and Rusyn brothers and sisters in Transcarpathia."

Hungarians and Rusyns aren't the only minorities in Transcarpathia who may be concerned about rising Ukrainian nationalism. Take, for example, the Roma or Gypsies who are poorly integrated into society and suffer from prejudice. When Gypsies are discriminated against, Pilash says, "They wind up not sending their kids to school. This lends itself to even greater exclusion. The Roma try to secure financial assistance from the government in the form of child support. Meanwhile, Gypsies perform the most menial and low-paying jobs. What's more, many people don't grasp the Gypsy nomadic lifestyle."

## Fanning the Flames

Rusyns and Hungarians certainly deserve autonomy, though hopefully both will firmly reject outside rightwing meddling by the likes of Jobbik. Fortunately, the Budapest protest at the Foreign Ministry wasn't too large --- just 200-300 people showed up. Nevertheless, Jobbik cannot be entirely dismissed: in April, 2014 the party placed third in Hungary's elections for the European Parliament and polled a full 20% of the vote. As such Jobbik, whose members dress in Nazi-like uniforms, has some influence on the overall political narrative in Hungary. Indeed, Hungarian Prime Minister Viktor Orbán is a staunch nationalist and his conservative Fidesz party competes with Jobbik for right wing votes.

Meanwhile, Hungarian Foreign Minister János Martonyi traveled to the Transcarpathian city of Uzhhorod and remarked "Transcarpathia's troubled ethnic Hungarian minority has to face new dangers but Hungary will not leave any insult at them unanswered." The *Guardian* of London notes that "Orbán thrives on conflict. He has used the many attacks on him – not least from the European commission – to justify what critics correctly see as a comprehensive attempt to undermine checks and balances, and remake the entire country in the image of one political party. According to Orbán, only Fidesz truly represents the nation; to be against Fidesz is not to be properly Hungarian."

Orbán has told lawmakers that he believes ethnic Hungarians are entitled to dual citizenship, and the Prime Minister has remarked that Ukraine must observe "community rights" of local Hungarians. If Kiev fails to observe such community rights, Orbán states, Hungary would have a "legitimate reason to be worried." When he was asked what he meant by "community rights," Orbán was vague and replied that Hungarians of Transcarpathia would themselves decide what rights they wanted to pursue. Hopefully, Orbán will not rile the waters much further in Transcarpathia, though the Prime Minister may be pushed to the right by Jobbik. In fact, the far right party has released a statement remarking that the party is "dumbfounded" by Orbán's move to recognize the post-Maidan government in Kiev, which represents a "threat" to the Hungarian minority. Moreover, Jobbik "demands" that Budapest take measures to "protect" the Hungarians in Ukraine and calls on Orbán to abandon its "submissive" attitude toward the west while standing up for ethnic Hungarians.

Recent developments suggest Orbán may be caving in to base and far right impulses. Budapest, in fact, has reportedly been handing out passports to Hungarian compatriots in Transcarpathia. In an effort to absorb as many Hungarians as possible, the Orbán government has lowered the bar: under the rules, applicants are only required to demonstrate mastery over the Hungarian language and possess at least one distant Hungarian relative. Needless to say, such moves come as an affront to Kiev which strictly prohibits dual citizenship. While it's unclear how many Transcarpathians have obtained Hungarian passports, the number may be in the tens of thousands.

According to Pilash, Ukrainians of Hungarian descent watch TV and read newspapers emanating from Budapest. "They are only loosely integrated into society," the activist adds, "and in general they haven't been very pro-Ukrainian. Hungarian peasant mothers from Transcarpthia staged protests in support of their sons who had been conscripted into the Ukrainian army.

In the midst of war with Russian separatists in the east, many young men didn't want to be shipped out." Within this volatile mix, Orbán has cultivated ties to none other than Vladimir Putin who already seeks effective partition of Ukraine. Indeed, the Hungarian Prime Minister opposes Western sanctions against Moscow which had been imposed after Russian annexation of Crimea. Moreover, Hungary relies heavily upon Russia for its oil and gas needs, and Orbán has signed a loan agreement with the Kremlin to upgrade a nuclear power plant.

In cozying up to Putin, Orbán is merely following in the footsteps of far right Jobbik. Party leader Vona, in fact, has traveled to Russia in order to meet with Russian nationalist Aleksandr Dugin, a key architect of conservative "Eurasian" ideology. Dugin supports the notion of Ukraine's "decomposition" into several parts with some areas being annexed by Russia (Transcarpathia, however, is considered too alien for Dugin so presumably the region could be absorbed by Hungary). Márton Gyöngyösi, Jobbik's deputy leader, has remarked that Hungary "should make alliances with all the countries that have ethnic minorities in Ukraine," adding that "Russia could be our ally."

During his stay in Moscow, Vona additionally met with Russia Duma leaders, and there have been "persistent rumors that Jobbik's enthusiasm is paid for with Russian rubles." Jobbik later characterized Vona's trip as "a major breakthrough as it became clear that Russian leaders consider Jobbik as a partner." A Jobbik report on the trip goes on to note that the U.S. is the "deformed offspring of Europe," and the E.U. is the "traitor of our continent." Reportedly, Vona hates the E.U. so much that he advocates Hungary joining Putin's Eurasian Union. Jobbik has additionally praised Russia's "exemplary" referendum in Crimea and the party even sent election observers to validate the results.

When I asked Pilash whether there was any concrete evidence Putin had stirred up ethnic separatism in the region, the activist responded, "Of course some groups oppose Ukraine and seek outside assistance from the Kremlin. In one case, a priest from the city of Uzhorod was tried for allegedly paying off separatists. There's also a strange man in Slovakia who calls himself the prime minister of Carpathian Rusyns. He has participated in pro-Russian international events, and perhaps the Kremlin provides him with tickets so he can travel to Moscow or the Crimea."

How do ethnic minorities in Transcarpathia perceive all this crass geopolitical maneuvering, as well as resurgent Ukrainian nationalism? Pilash, who generally eschews ethnic labels and considers himself more of an internationalist, declares "I define myself as a Rusyn from Ruthenia, though I also have Hungarian, Croatian, and perhaps German, Tatar and Jewish roots. At home I converse in Rusyn with my family, though I also speak Hungarian." According to Pilash, Transcarpathia is a very tolerant region and "there's not a lot of interest in right wing activities." For the moment, at least, the activist believes Rusyns aren't headed for any kind of major confrontation with the Ukrainian state.

Nevertheless, Pilash says outward expressions of nationalism at Maidan made him feel somewhat strange. The main stage on the square, he declares, was occupied by the mainstream opposition and there was "a lot of foolishness, including nationalist slogans, nationalist music, and prayers held every hour." There is general support in Transcarpathia for greater autonomy, says Pilash, which must not be confused with secession. In 1991, after the collapse of the Soviet Union, Transcarpathia held a referendum and seventy percent of respondents voted in favor of autonomy. In the event that Ukraine disintegrates, then, "some say we can always join Hungary or Slovakia."

CHAPTER 8

# Religion and Cultural Conservatism

DURING MY TRIP TO KIEV, I was struck by mementoes placed in and around Kiev's Maidan square. The plaques featured individual photo portraits of fallen martyrs --- the so-called "Heavenly Hundred" who had sacrificed their lives during violent protests against Yanukovych. What particularly got my attention about these mementoes was the overt display of religious iconography. Lying alongside the photos, Ukrainians had laid rosary beads, framed religious images of Christ and other memorabilia. Taken together, the photos and other donated items took on the look of shrines.

While some have sought to interpret the overall political meaning of revolution on the Maidan, few have dwelled upon underlying religious connotations. To be sure, Ukraine isn't as religious as Russia but nevertheless the Church plays a significant role in society. No one church dominates in Ukraine, with various branches including the Ukrainian Orthodox Church (linked to the Patriarchate of Moscow), the Patriarchate of Kiev and the Ukrainian Autocephalous Orthodox Church all holding sway. Though the Orthodox Church is the largest faith, other groups include the Ukrainian Greek-Catholic Church and the Roman Catholic Church.

Activist Gorbach of Autonomous Workers' Union says the larger Ukrainian Orthodox Church has historically displayed backward and retrograde ideas. "They have their own agenda," he remarked, "which is socially conservative, racist against blacks and all non-Slavic peoples --- though they wouldn't have any big problems with Germans or British --- anti-Semitic and homophobic." Gorbach adds for good measure that the hardcore Orthodox Church opposes "rotten western values and multiculturalism." For a more complete view, I head over to Kiev's old Jewish quarter of Podil, where Zissels of the Euro-Asian Jewish Congress confirms that the Ukrainian Church of the Moscow Patriarchate is "the most anti-Semitic amongst the churches." Zissels says anti-Semitic literature has even been sold at such churches. He adds, however, that there's little evidence of such virulent anti-Semitism within other Orthodox branches of the church.

## Museum Controversy

Larissa Babij, an American of Ukrainian descent who moved to Kiev in 2005, works as an arts curator. Babij never really saw herself as a political activist, but when she observed how Ukrainians had little sway over their own cultural institutions she helped to found an outfit called Art Workers' Self Defense Initiative. The original group was comprised of between ten and twenty people, many of whom knew each other personally and had collaborated over the years. Since the breakup of the old Soviet Union, Babij told me, there's been a kind of ideological vacuum in Ukraine and a counter-reaction to earlier forced atheism characteristic of Communist rule. As a result, some have turned to religion as a source of solace.

During the Yanukovych era, Babij remarked, there was a rather incestuous relationship between church and state. In July, 2013 Kiev's Mystetskyi Arsenal art museum put on a show titled "The Great and the Grand." The exhibit was called to celebrate the 1025th anniversary of the baptism of Kievan Rus, the original medieval state considered to be the Orthodox foundation of Ukraine, Belarus and Russia. In a very symbolic sense, the show was designed to foster closer cultural ties between Ukraine and Russia. What is more, Yanukovych exercised great influence over Arsenal, a museum which lacked its own political autonomy even though the institution is state-funded and receives taxpayer money.

When it became clear the show would be partially funded by top-ranking clergy associated with none other than the Ukrainian Orthodox Church, Babij grew concerned. Could the president be seeking to perpetuate his own state ideology favoring closer ties to the Church? As suspicions grew, a controversy erupted at the museum which eroded Arsenal's already fast deteriorating reputation. On the night prior to Yanukovych's personal visit to the museum, Arsenal's director literally took a can of black paint and doused one of the exhibit's art works which she deemed immoral.

The work in question, a mural depicting a flaming nuclear reactor with priests and judges partially immersed in a vat of red liquid, soon became a cause célèbre as Kiev's arts community rushed to the defense of creative self-expression. Prior to the opening, eight activists were arrested outside the museum protesting the creeping consolidation of church and state. In defending her controversial decision, Arsenal's director claimed the exhibit "should inspire pride in the state." She added, "If you participate in [an] exhibition dedicated to the 1025th anniversary of the baptism of Kievan Rus, you don't have to do your best to offend the faithful, to lower the reputation of all clergy." In the wake of the controversy, Arsenal's deputy director resigned in protest, while some suggested the director had come under pressure to eliminate controversial work in advance of Yanukovych's visit.

As the controversy grew more heated, Babij's Art Workers' Self-Defense Initiative called for an outright boycott of Arsenal until the museum agreed to safeguard creative self-expression. Curiously, however, the guarded local arts community failed to rally behind such calls, and even backed Arsenal. At the time, Babij noted that boycotters were criticized "for being unconstructive, ineffective, and focusing on their international image at the expense of loyalty to local institutions." Nikita Kadan, a local artist, said the entire situation "was awfully similar to Soviet-era public, collective-shaming tactics, through which cultural actors were compelled to participate and atone for their transgressions." When asked why the boycott didn't receive more grass-roots support, Babij remarked "fear is such a driving force here in Ukraine. If I say something against this institution, there's a fear of losing opportunities. If I offend someone, I won't be able to show my work at Arsenal. And if I never show at Arsenal, then how will I advance my career?"

## RELIGION ON THE MAIDAN

Though certainly disconcerting, the Arsenal controversy did not lead to a consolidation of church and state though perhaps, if he had not been toppled from power, Yanukovych would have sought greater ties along these lines. As Ukraine veered into political turbulence on the Maidan, a fractured church with its many denominations was forced to take sides. Historically, the Orthodox faith has placed greater emphasis on backing up state authority, rather than supporting the aspirations of civil society. With Yanukovych clinging to power, however, top clergy was placed in an uncomfortable bind.

The Ukrainian Orthodox Church, with its ties to the Moscow Patriarchate and upper echelons of Russian political and ecclesiastical leadership, found itself in a particularly problematic conundrum. As events unfolded, top clergy sought to remain neutral in the midst of crisis. Maintaining such neutrality proved difficult, however, since many members of the Ukrainian Orthodox Church were themselves pro-Western. Though the church was eventually obliged to back Maidan protesters and Poroshenko, it did so belatedly. Other denominations got out in front of Maidan protests much earlier, however. According to Zissels of Euro-Asian Jewish Congress, the Greek Catholic Church was the most influential religious grouping on the Maidan.

Gradually, religious leaders began to assume more importance during demonstrations. When riot police attacked protesters, scattering a whopping 10,000 people, many sought refuge in nearby St. Michael's Golden-Domed Monastery. There, demonstrators were protected by local monks affiliated with the Ukrainian Orthodox Church's Patriarchate of Kiev. Several days later, when riot police attacked again, a graduate student at a nearby theology school began to ring sacred bells located next to a local cathedral. The noise and commotion could be heard for miles, and in response to the call, priests dressed in cassocks stood between riot police and protesters in an effort to restore peace. Later, police withdrew without resorting to further violence.

Meanwhile, priests led daily prayers at the barricades. In the middle of the square, a Greek Catholic Church chapel provided daily Mass, confession and even counseling. At night, priests from all faiths led a prayer after crowds recited the national anthem. Such developments began to raise eyebrows amongst Ukrainian progressives, however. At a certain point, Babij told me, prayers were literally being recited on the hour at Maidan. "It was definitely uncomfortable for those of us who weren't really religious in that way," she said. All of a sudden, she added, religion became very dominant and "Maidan took on a homogeneity which might have been representative of the majority, or maybe representative of what some people thought the majority should be. But it definitely was not all-inclusive. It definitely had those patriotic, religious and nationalistic overtones."

Despite pronounced religious nationalism at Maidan, some believe there is little danger Ukraine will somehow merge church and state. Danilchenko of the Euro-Asian Jewish Congress believes the Orthodox faith doesn't inform Ukrainian nationalism to the same degree as Russian nationalism. "In Ukraine," he told me, "faith is more of a personal affair. You don't hear slogans like 'We are Ukraine, we are Orthodox!'" Danilchenko adds that many Ukrainians simply see themselves as European and prefer a strong separation between church and state. In Russia by contrast, "it doesn't work that way. The country has a state religion which is almost akin to Saudi Arabia." Babij concedes that Ukraine is definitely more secular than Russia. After observing political controversies at the Arsenal museum, however, the curator isn't under any great illusions. In the long-term, she adds, Ukraine still "has all the potential to go in the direction of Russia from a religious standpoint."

A religious memento near Maidan square.

What is the role of religion within the new Ukraine?

At mementos to the fallen around Maidan square, religion and politics mix.

# ART AND CULTURE IN THE POST-MAIDAN *MILIEU*

To what extent can the EuroMaidan movement be seen as a reaction against the stultifying cultural *milieu* within Ukraine? "I definitely would not call Euromaidan a counter-cultural movement," Babij noted emphatically while letting out a chuckle. On the other hand, she remarks, EuroMaidan "held the potential for a future counter-culture. The way Maidan evolved and the spontaneous manner in which people came together and collaborated was really something new." To the outside observer, Maidan itself may have seemed like something of an open canvas displaying street theater and props for example. Indeed, one art collective called Mistetska Sotnya performed a variety of different street shows featuring musicians, circus acrobats and ballerinas. Somewhat audaciously, performers carried out their shows while standing right up against the barricades. Meanwhile, artists decorated shields and helmets which belonged to anti-Yanukovych fighters. Maidan's creative output wasn't simply limited to street theater, however, but also included posters, photography and ornamental painting. Protests also spurred growth of documentary film, while noted musicians played a piano which had been painted blue and yellow.

On the other hand, though certainly prodigious and impressive, Maidan's creative outpouring was not always associated with "counter-culture." Indeed, art took on a nationalist or rightist complexion in some cases. Take, for example, the emergence of so-called "zhlob" artists allied to the far right. According to Babij, zhlob artists are "intentionally low-brow," "very aggressive," and populist. In one gallery exhibit, zhlob artists literally placed a couple of Russians inside a cage. Later, on the Maidan, zhlob artists had their own tent which served as a makeshift gallery. During anti-Yanukovych protests, rightist artists sought to demonstrate their patriotism by accusing other artists, particularly those on the progressive left, of not being sufficiently politically active.

In a local Kiev café, Babij elucidated her own skeptical cultural perspective. In the winter and spring of 2014, she said, "Something really changed in Ukraine. There was a potential for a revolution. In the end though it turned out to be a circular revolution where you come back to a certain point where you started out." Indeed, the curator noted, Ukraine became awash in nationalism which could hinder the emergence of a more progressive arts scene. "In general," she declared, "the Ukrainian public has a pretty simplistic idea of culture. I don't think political parties for that matter share any well articulated cultural policies." Rather than Maidan reverberating throughout wider society, "It's more like Maidan took place and arts institutions continue to think in the same way as they did before. Within this context, Maidan simply becomes another 'theme.' There's a Maidan museum where they exhibit artifacts. Maidan objects have been 'fetishized' and painted helmets are displayed to the public. Unfortunately, however, we've already forgotten what Maidan was originally about."

CHAPTER 9

# LGBT and Women

THOUGH IT'S NOT COMMONLY KNOWN, Ukraine's LGBT community played a significant role in the Maidan revolution. Careful not to alienate conservative nationalist elements, LGBT protesters tactfully avoided promoting their cause openly. According to E.U. Observer, LGBT activists refrained from brandishing their own slogans and banners lest they provoke homophobic violence. The Observer remarks that "during the revolution, the LGBT community behaved courageously, but also pragmatically: it didn't champion the rights of the gay minority in order not to split Maidan into liberal and illiberal factions."

In the wake of Maidan, however, many within the LGBT community feel betrayed by the very revolution which they helped to spearhead in the first place. In Ukraine, much of the talk revolves around repelling Putin and Russian-backed separatists, rather than adhering to liberal-minded values. It's an ironic coda to the Maidan, which was initially driven forward by pro-Western and progressive sentiment. Judging from recent events, however, it would appear that Maidan's liberal credo was always rather skin deep. Indeed, many conservative Ukrainians seem to have fallen back on a common refrain: don't resort to criticism of our country's internal politics, for such "divisive" tactics will only serve to embolden the Kremlin. What is more, political elites have desperately sought to outmaneuver the LGBT community by playing the nationalist card.

It's bad enough when right wing nationalists espouse homophobic views, but arguably even worse when such notions are sanctioned at the top.

According to activists, authorities told the LGBT community the government was unable to introduce significant hate crime or discrimination legislation due to Ukraine's "critical situation of conflict with Russia." A recent report from National Public Radio quotes one activist who declares "the public discourse [in Ukraine] has said, 'Look, you are not important right now. We cannot discuss gay issues…Stop talking about it.' It's all about the war."

Ukrainian excuses on the LGBT question reached ridiculous new heights in advance of a planned Pride march in Kiev last year. Prior to the event, activists sought a meeting with Mayor Vitaly Klitschko in order to secure vital police protection. Rather questionably, Klitschko refused while concocting absurdist, far-fetched explanations. It wasn't the right time to hold Pride, the mayor claimed, since Ukraine was in the midst of war and the public didn't have a clear grasp of homosexuality. Providing police protection to the Pride march, the mayor said, would furthermore represent a needless "provocation" toward Russia, a country which has very strict anti-LGBT laws. In making such declarations, Klischko echoes the mindset of other conservative politicians. For some time, Russia has pushed its own propaganda focusing on the west's so-called tolerance of "sexual perversions," and Kremlin media even refers to Europe as "Gayropa." Rather than seeking to deflect such rhetoric, Ukrainian authorities have reacted defensively. Apparently, Kiev is concerned that drawing attention to LGBT rights would only help Russian separatists and alienate domestic conservative groups.

## Gay Pride Fiasco

For the LGBT community, securing armed protection is hardly some kind of unnecessary or idle pastime. In 2012, local authorities similarly withdrew their promise to protect participants at Pride celebrations. Later, organizers were obliged to cancel the parade out of security concerns. The following year, Pride went ahead but only under heavy police guard and the proceedings lasted a mere hour. In light of the adverse security environment, Klitschko moved to cancel Pride in 2014. While concerns over public safety are surely warranted, the mayor failed to demonstrate any understanding of the LGBT community, remarking that the parade essentially amounted to a mere "entertainment event" rather than a vehicle designed to promote human rights. With no support emanating from the mayor's office, and fearful at the prospect of far right street violence, organizers were similarly forced to cancel their parade.

It looked like history would repeat itself once again, but at long last security was provided last year when Klitschko relented and agreed to provide a 1,500 police escort. Even so, the parade took place within an atmosphere of fear and intimidation and LGBT activists distributed flyers on how to protect oneself from beatings and gas attacks during Pride. It turns out such fears were not unfounded: unidentified assailants threw stones and smoke bombs during the event. After attackers hurled nail-studded firecrackers, one policeman was sent to hospital. In the end, the march only lasted a mere 20 minutes. It seems likely the assailants were affiliated with so-called Right Sektor, a group which had threatened to provoke hostilities prior to Gay Pride.

On the surface at least, it's pretty easy to point the finger at right wing street toughs. In fact, attacks at Pride were hardly isolated and anti-LGBT violence committed by nationalist groups has recently increased. Since the Maidan revolution such groups have grown ever more powerful. It's reportedly gotten so dangerous for LGBT activists that some gays have sought diplomatic asylum in the U.S. A video experiment conducted in Kiev illuminates the depths of the problem. In an effort to test the waters, two gay men strolled down the streets in broad daylight, hand-in-hand. The pair then sat down on a bench on Khreschatyk, a central street near Maidan square. Rather ominously, a gang of young men quickly encircled the two and asked the men if they were patriots. Moments later, the gang squirted pepper spray in the gay men's faces and kicked the couple.

As if that were not enough, it also seems right wing nationalists were responsible for launching an attack on the Zhovten or October Theater in November, 2014. Zhovten is Kiev's oldest theater and a favorite among art buffs. During the annual Molodist film festival, Zhovten screened a new

French film about a married man who dresses up as a woman. About a hundred members of Kiev's LGBT community showed up for the premiere. Twenty minutes into the movie, a loud noise like exploding firecrackers --- probably an incendiary grenade --- sent people scrambling into a panic. Though fire engines later showed up, much of the theater was destroyed in a blaze. Fortunately, there were no casualties but the incident sent a chilling message to the LGBT community. Later, two men were apprehended and admitted they had aimed to disrupt the event out of contempt for gay people. Two days later, Right Sektor again tried to shut down another LGBT film screening. Though certainly troubling, these incidents are hardly isolated: as early as 2009, prior to the Maidan revolution, Kiev art gallery Ya was set on fire following the presentation of a gay literary anthology.

## Still Not Fully European

While no one is letting right wing nationalists off the hook, blaming such groups for the rise in homophobia misses the point. Gay rights activists, in fact, have questioned police commitment to keep them safe. Though the security forces captured arsonists involved in the Zhovten blaze, officials were unable to prosecute the individuals for hate crimes since Ukraine lacks legislation which specifically protects people based on sexual orientation. In the event, the authorities wound up prosecuting the perpetrators based on mere hooliganism. Moreover, in the wake of last year's Gay Pride fiasco, police failed to bring all suspected attackers to court. Some have expressed doubts that the official investigation will yield tangible result, and LGBT activists have even floated the idea that law enforcement might have been complicit in the attacks, noting that right wing toughs display an uncanny knack of locating gay pride marches at the spur of the moment, despite last minute changes.

Meanwhile, Kiev's political elite has been reluctant to criticize the far right which is seen as patriotic in the fight against Russian-backed separatists. Members of the LGBT community argue that politicians have helped to foster an air of impunity toward right wing extremism which has only served to embolden fringe elements. Take, for example Mayor Klitschko, a former hero of the Maidan revolution. When asked how he would respond to the Zhovten attack, Klischko answered blandly that human rights were a good thing but he would not "stand up for gays and lesbians." Moreover, though the new government has placed significant importance on joining the so-called Schengen zone (a club of E.U. nations which allows for visa and passport-free travel), the Ukrainian parliament recently scuppered any such possibility when it blocked legislation which would have banned discrimination against LGBT people in the workplace.

Previously, the E.U. had warned Ukraine that it should amend its antiquated labor code which fails to prohibit discrimination against gays. In the Ukrainian parliament, only 117 legislators voted for changes demanded by Brussels, while nationalists and populists resoundingly defeated the measure with 343 votes. The vote sent a chill through the LGBT community, which already feels threatened and abandoned. In a recent survey, a whopping 65 percent of Ukrainian gays said they faced infringements on their rights, including verbal abuse, intimidation and loss of employment or even direct physical violence. In light of historic failures on the Maidan, many within the LGBT community may wonder if and when another revolution will eventually spearhead the protections which they most desperately seek.

It would appear that Ukraine likes the idea of being a part of Europe, but is reluctant to embrace underlying Western European values. "It's worth recalling," notes E.U. Observer, "that the Euromaidan began because the former regime declined to sign an association treaty with the E.U. and was about to somersault Ukraine into the Russian world." Nevertheless, Ukrainian politicians are only willing to move the country so far. An article in *Foreign Policy* magazine quotes one gay refugee from war-torn eastern Ukraine who remarks "there are some people who just want to join 'Europe' without changing their values and without understanding what it all means. But if people really want to change our country, the change has to start within them and their relationship to others."

# Women on the Maidan

So much for the LGBT community, but what about women? During anti-Yanukovych demonstrations, it became clear women were to play a key role in spearheading revolt. Indeed, some estimate that almost half of Maidan protesters were women. Out on the square, women attended to the wounded; published newspapers; wrote articles; aided journalists through translation services; organized screenings of documentary films (and actually filmed their own documentaries about women's struggle); organized rallies, and prepared food staples like borscht. Meanwhile, one young woman pleaded for international help in a video posted to YouTube entitled "I am the Ukrainian." "We are civilized," the woman remarks, "but our government are barbarians." The video was viewed millions of times and amassed tens of thousands of comments.

Maidan broke down gender stereotypes in important ways. Though women took on some traditional roles, they also shook up the *status quo* by directly participating on the front lines. *Elle* magazine notes that women donned gas masks, helmets, padded vests and camouflage jackets while fighting alongside men. In addition, women prepared Molotov cocktails and brought them to the front lines, while a women's brigade trained in self-defense tactics. According to activist Neshevets, men and women on the independent left made a conscious effort to avoid sexism. Nevertheless, she adds, "sometimes you realize you can't change everything in one day."

Neshevets remarks that sexism did in fact rear its head at Maidan. The prevailing attitude, she says, was more or less like "'Woman come here! Smile and support the fighters.'" Alternatively men would shout out, "'Woman, come here to prepare some cookies, snacks and tea! Woman, you see how fighters are resting now so go and clean up!'" It was also frustrating, Neshevets says, to observe how men tended to dominate political discussion. On the other hand, she concedes, women were sometimes shy or afraid to speak up in a public forum. The dynamic posed a thorny problem, since "you can't force someone to talk." Nevertheless, Neshevets and others managed to include women at conference panels in an effort to promote greater gender equality.

On a certain level, reports of sexism are surprising in light of Ukrainian history. The country is home to various women's rights groups including FEMEN, a radical outfit whose members bear their breasts to protest sex trafficking and domestic abuse. Declaring that "Ukraine is not a brothel," FEMEN rose to notoriety by denouncing a New Zealand radio show host who promised local men they would be provided with local wives if they traveled to Ukraine. Since then, FEMEN has taken on other controversial subjects ranging from organized religion (members are militant atheists), to corruption and patriarchy in all forms.

The arrival of FEMEN caps off recent history which has seen slow and steady progress for women. During the Soviet period, all women had equal rights (at least officially) and also enjoyed equal access to education and jobs. In the post-Soviet era, some women have been successful in government and business. Take, for example, former Prime Minister Yulia Tymoshenko, who was a prominent businesswoman before entering politics. On the other hand, Ukraine is a very traditional and patriarchal society and Tymoshenko may represent the minority. Even though women are more educated than men on average, they are under-represented in leadership positions. In fact, though many women work in government itself, few are elected to office. Meanwhile, though Ukraine has anti-discrimination laws on the books, such measures are rarely enforced. Chauvinist attitudes have sometimes been placed on vivid display, for example in 2010 when Yanukovych famously refused to participate in a debate with Tymoshenko. Yanukovych, who was then running for president, claimed that his opponent's proper place was "in the kitchen."

## Women's Rights in Post-Maidan *Milieu*

Given all these obstacles, what can women expect from the post-Maidan *milieu*? Speaking with Neshevets about the situation proves sobering. Maidan, she remarks, was a brief window in time and "it will take decades to achieve anyone's rights, let alone women's rights." The activist adds that war with

Russian-backed separatists has diverted attention from gender equality, and "of course the media exacerbates the problem by talking about the war all the time while all other problems are minimized. In this manner, feminist issues become invisible." Meanwhile, though women figured prominently at Maidan, Ukraine is hardly on the path toward radical feminist revolution. In fact, FEMEN played little or no role at Maidan, having been previously subjected to a campaign of harassment and repression under the Yanukovych regime. Furthermore, activists were obliged to close their offices in Ukraine simply out of fear of reprisals. In the wake of Maidan, FEMEN has returned to Ukraine though it's unclear whether society is ready for the group's particular brand of firebrand politics.

According to London's *Independent*, FEMEN has been criticized for protesting too many wide-ranging issues as well as "for their trademark topless tactics, which opponents say buy into the degrading sexualized tropes they claim to be fighting against." Additionally, FEMEN has taken on strident anti-religious tactics and in one case a member even cut into a wooden cross with a chainsaw. The act reportedly lost FEMEN some supporters and placed the group at odds with many in wider society. In the wake of the Soviet Union's collapse and accompanying ideological vacuum, some women are apparently embracing religious faith as well as older gender stereotypes of motherhood.

But while Ukraine may not be wholeheartedly ready for the likes of FEMEN, women have made modest gains since Maidan. In fact, the public has even elected young women to parliament who are intent on abolishing age-old kleptocracy. In an effort to improve transparency, some women politicians seek to make laws pertaining to alimony payments more efficient and less corrupt. At a more basic and fundamental level, however, newly elected MP's face an uphill battle since many backward male colleagues may still believe that women ought to be relegated to the home.

A politicized portrait on the Maidan of Lesya Ukrainka, a noted Ukrainian woman essayist, poet, dramatist and critic of the late nineteenth and early twentieth centuries. A Marxist, she opposed the Czarist regime and translated the *Communist Manifesto* into Ukrainian. The caption reads "Whoever frees himself will be free."

# Sources

✤

## Prologue

Evan McMurry, "Sen. McCain: Russia is a 'Gas Station Masquerading as a Country'" Mediaite, March 16, 2014, http://www.mediaite.com/tv/sen-mccain-russia-is-a-gas-station-masquerading-as-a-country/

Nikolas Kozloff, "Interview: What Can Be Expected From Ukrainian Right in the Midst of Political and Military Crisis?" Huffington Post, July 30, 2014, http://www.nikolaskozloff.com/blog.htm?post=964962

Nikolas Kozloff, "Ukraine: Enough with Stale Insider Debates in the Media," Huffington Post, March 12, 2015, http://www.nikolaskozloff.com/blog.htm?post=988626

Nikolas Kozloff, "Welcome to Ukraine: One of the 'Biggest Kleptocracies in the World'" Huffington Post, February 15, 2015, http://www.nikolaskozloff.com/blog.htm?post=985316

Nikolas Kozloff, "Coming of Age: Ukraine's Maidan Student Generation Assesses Next Moves," Huffington Post, February 5, 2015, http://www.nikolaskozloff.com/blog.htm?post=984076

Nikolas Kozloff, "Note to Ukraine: Stop Whitewashing the Political Record," Huffington Post, January 23, 2015, http://www.nikolaskozloff.com/blog. htm?post=982461

Nikolas Kozloff, "Ukraine: Insider Oligarchs Derail Maidan Revolution," Huffington Post, February 27, 2015, http://www.nikolaskozloff.com/blog. htm?post=987073

## Chapter 1: EuroMaidan and the Independent Left

Nikolas Kozloff, "What Can Be Expected From Ukrainian Right in the Midst of Political and Military Crisis?" Huffington Post, July 30, 2014, http://www. nikolaskozloff.com/blog.htm?post=964962

Nikolas Kozloff, "Ukraine Crisis: Time for Thorough Overhaul of the International Left," Huffington Post, March 20, 2014, http://www.nikolas-kozloff.com/blog.htm?post=951341

Serhiy Kvit, "Student groups have vital role to play in universities and society," *University World News*, August, 2012, http://www.universityworldnews.com/ article.php?story=2012081513363667

Nikolas Kozloff, "In Midst of War, Ukrainian Political Left Ponders Next Moves," Huffington Post, January 5, 2015, http://www.nikolaskozloff.com/ blog.htm?post=980568

Nikolas Kozloff, "Maidan One Year Later: What Happened to the Social Component?" Huffington Post, January 28, 2015, http://www.nikolaskozloff. com/blog.htm?post=982938

Patrick Smith, "Ukraine Starts Its March to Free-Market Capitalism," *Fiscal Times,* December 15, 2014 http://www.thefiscaltimes.com/Columns/2014/12/15/ Ukraine-Starts-Its-March-Free-Market-Capitalism

Emily Channell-Justice, "Flexibility and Fragmentation: Student Activism and Ukraine's (Euro)Maidan Protests," *Berkeley Journal of Sociology*, October 20, 2014, http://berkeleyjournal.org/2014/10/flexibility-and-fragmentation-student-activism-and-ukraines-euromaidan-protests/

LeftEast (online left journal),"Manifesto: 10 Theses of the Leftist Opposition in Ukraine," January 14, 2014, http://www.criticatac.ro/lefteast/manifesto-left-opposition-in-ukraine/

Nikolas Kozloff, "Coming of Age: Ukraine's Maidan Student Generation Assesses Next Moves," Huffington Post, February 5, 2015, http://www.nikolaskozloff.com/blog.htm?post=984076

## Chapter 2: Disillusionment and War

Nikolas Kozloff, "In Midst of War, Ukrainian Political Left Ponders Next Moves," Huffington Post, January 5, 2015, http://www.nikolaskozloff.com/blog.htm?post=980568

Nikolas Kozloff, "Coming of Age: Ukraine's Maidan Student Generation Assesses Next Moves," Huffington Post, February 5, 2015, http://www.nikolaskozloff.com/blog.htm?post=984076

Nikolas Kozloff, "Note to Ukraine: Stop Whitewashing the Political Record," Huffington Post, January 23, 2015, http://www.nikolaskozloff.com/blog.htm?post=982461

David Stern, "Ukraine underplays role of far right in conflict," BBC, December 13, 2014, http://www.bbc.com/news/world-europe-30414955

# Chapter 3: Oligarchs and Populists

Transparency International, "A year after Maidan, Ukraine is still the most corrupt country in Europe," December 3, 2014, http://www.transparency.org/news/pressrelease/a_year_after_maidan_ukraine_is_still_the_most_corrupt_country_in_europe

Janek Lasocki, "Whatever happened to (Euro) Maidan," Open Democracy, October 6, 2014, https://www.opendemocracy.net/od-russia/janek-lasocki/whatever-happened-to-euro-maidan

Mark Snowiss, "Ukraine's Euromaidan Reforms Reveal Deep Divisions," Voice of America News, October 20, 2014, http://www.voanews.com/content/ukraine-euromaidan-reforms-reveal-deep-divisions/2487297.html

"The curse of corruption in Ukraine: Ostrich zoo and vintage cars," *Economist*, June 14, 2014, http://www.economist.com/news/europe/21604234-fight-against-corruption-steep-uphill-battle-ostrich-zoo-and-vintage-cars

Devin Ackles, "Ukraine's Epic War On Corruption, Explained." Medium, November 28, 2014, https://medium.com/@Hromadske/ukraines-epic-war-on-corruption-explained-73dfab93fbf0#.wdjxvpbcj

Petro Poroshenko, "A Year Later, a New Ukraine," *Wall Street Journal*, December 4, 2014, http://www.wsj.com/articles/petro-poroshenko-a-year-later-a-new-ukraine-1417738446

Nikolas Kozloff, "Ukraine: Nationalist Flags, Insignia and Curious Symbolism," Huffington Post, January 16, 2015, http://www.nikolaskozloff.com/blog.htm?post=981824

"Profile: Ukraine's President Petro Poroshenko," BBC, June 7, 2014, http://www.bbc.com/news/world-europe-26822741

"Ukraine's renewed anti-corruption fight looks promising so far – at least on paper," *Kyiv Post*, October 22, 2014, http://www.kyivpost.com/article/content/ukraine/ukraines-renewed-anti-corruption-fight-looks-promising-so-far-at-least-on-paper-369014.html

Oleksandr Savochenko, "Ukraine economy minister resigns over state corruption," Agence France Presse, February 3, 2016, https://www.yahoo.com/news/ukraine-economy-minister-resigns-citing-stalled-reforms-100959978.html

Sophie Pinkham, "Which Ukraine?" *New Yorker*, February 12, 2015, http://www.newyorker.com/news/news-desk/ukraine

Oliver Bullough, "Welcome to Ukraine, the most corrupt nation in Europe," *Guardian*, February 6, 2015, http://www.theguardian.com/news/2015/feb/04/welcome-to-the-most-corrupt-nation-in-europe-ukraine

"Not enough," *Kyiv Post*, November 28, 2014, http://www.kyivpost.com/opinion/editorial/not-enough-373377.html

Patrick Smith, "Ukraine's Second Front: Obama and Kerry Are Now at War With Europe," *Fiscal Times*, February 9, 2015, http://www.thefiscaltimes.com/Columns/2015/02/09/Ukraines-Second-Front-Obama-and-Kerry-Are-Now-War-Europe

Stratfor, "Crisis in Ukraine Shifts Some Oligarchs' Fates," January 26, 2015, https://www.stratfor.com/sample/analysis/crisis-ukraine-shifts-some-oligarchs-fates

Sergii Leshchenko, "Ukraine's Oligarchs Are Still Calling the Shots," *Foreign Policy*, August 14, 2014, http://foreignpolicy.com/2014/08/14/ukraines-oligarchs-are-still-calling-the-shots/

Avedis Hadjian, "Ukrainian Oligarchs Stay Above The Fray And Let The Crisis Play Out," *International Business Times*, February 26, 2014, http://www.ibtimes.com/ukrainian-oligarchs-stay-above-fray-let-crisis-play-out-1558121

Alec Luhn, "Return of the Oligarchs: Ukraine Poised to Elect 'Chocolate King' as President," *The Nation*, May 23, 2014, http://www.thenation.com/article/return-oligarchs-ukraine-poised-elect-chocolate-king-president/

Andrew Kramer, "Ukraine Turns to Its Oligarchs for Political Help," *New York Times*, March 2, 2014, http://www.nytimes.com/2014/03/03/world/europe/ukraine-turns-to-its-oligarchs-for-political-help.html?_r=2

Jeffrey Young, "Oligarchs Adapt to New Ukraine," Voice of America, April 28, 2014, http://www.voanews.com/content/oligarchs-adapt-to-the-new-ukraine/1901331.html

Adrian Karatnycky, "Warlords and armed groups threaten Ukraine's rebuilding," *Washington Post,* December 30, 2014, https://www.washingtonpost.com/opinions/the-rise-of-warlords-threatens-ukraines-recovery/2014/12/30/a23b2d36-8f7b-11e4-a412-4b735edc7175_story.html

Shaun Walker, "Caught between Russia and the US? The curious case of Ukraine's Dmytro Firtash," *Guardian*, January 23, 2016, http://www.theguardian.com/world/2016/jan/23/dmytro-firtash-ukraine-oligarch-exile-caught-between-russia-us

"Stay away Firtash," *Kyiv Post*, March 31, 2016, http://www.kyivpost.com/article/opinion/editorial/stay-away-firtash-411104.html

Eric Reguly, "The rise and fall of Ukrainian oligarch Dmitry Firtash," *The Globe and Mail*, April 19, 2014 http://www.theglobeandmail.com/report-on-business/international-business/european-business/the-rise-and-fall-of-ukrainian-oligarch-dmitry-firtash/article18067412/?page=all

Harriet Salem, "Ukraine's Oligarchs: A Who's Who Guide," Vice, October 13, 2014 https://news.vice.com/article/ukraines-oligarchs-a-whos-who-guide

Sabra Ayres, "Ukraine's oligarchs remain influential as ever," al-Jazeera America, June 21, 2014, http://america.aljazeera.com/articles/2014/6/21/ukraine-oligarchsinfluence.html

Christian Neef, "Yanukovych's Fall: The Power of Ukraine's Billionaires," *Der Spiegel,* February 25, 2014, http://www.spiegel.de/international/europe/how-oligarchs-in-ukraine-prepared-for-the-fall-of-yanukovych-a-955328.html

Nick Kochan, "Ukraine's oligarchs: who are they – and which side are they on?" *Guardian*, March 9, 2014, http://www.theguardian.com/world/shortcuts/2014/mar/09/ukraines-oligarchs-who-are-they-which-side-are-on

Cable from U.S. Embassy in Kiev, "UKRAINE: EXTREME MAKEOVER FOR THE PARTY OF REGIONS?" February 3, 2006, WikiLeaks web site, https://wikileaks.org/plusd/cables/06KIEV473_a.html

Leonid Bershidsky, "Ukraine's President Takes on Its Richest Man," Bloomberg, April 24, 2015, http://www.bloombergview.com/articles/2015-04-24/ukraine-s-president-takes-on-its-richest-man

Roman Olearchyk, "Kiev government looks to loosen oligarchs' grip in Ukraine," *Financial Times,* April 26, 2015, http://www.ft.com/cms/s/0/064d1392-e770-11e4-8ebb-00144feab7de.html

Nikolas Kozloff, "Welcome to Ukraine: One of the 'Biggest Kleptocracies in the World'" Huffington Post, February 15, 2015, http://www.nikolaskozloff.com/blog.htm?post=985316

Alan Cullison, "Ukraine's Secret Weapon: Feisty Oligarch Ihor Kolomoisky," *Wall Street Journal*, June 27, 2014, http://www.wsj.com/articles/ ukraines-secret-weapon-feisty-oligarch-ihor-kolomoisky-1403886665

Vladislav Davidzon, "Putin Defends Ukraine's Jews, Slams Ukraine's Jewish Oligarchs," *Tablet*, March 5, 2014, http://www.tabletmag.com/ scroll/165099/putin-defends-ukraines-jews-slams-ukraines-jewish-oligarchs

"Ukraine's future: President v oligarch," *Economist*, March 28, 2015, http:// www.economist.com/news/europe/21647355-building-nation-means- putting-plutocrats-their-place-president-v-oligarch

Charles McPhedran, "Thug Politics, Kiev," *Foreign Policy*, October 9, 2014, http://foreignpolicy.com/2014/10/09/thug-politics-kiev/

Yuras Karmanau, "Another faction quits Ukraine's governing coalition," Associated Press, February 18, 2016, http://www.businessinsider.com/ ap-another-faction-quits-ukraines-governing-coalition-2016-2

Robert Beckhusen, "Ukrainian Election's Real Losers—Far Right Parties," Medium, Oct 26, 2014, https://medium.com/war-is-boring/ukrainian- elections-real-losers-far-right-parties-94f4f7c0cdab#.my2j50j8q

Will Freeman, "How Corrupt Opportunists Could Win Big In Ukraine's Government Shake-Up," Think Progress, July 25, 2014, http://thinkprogress. org/world/2014/07/25/3463927/ukraine-government-problems/

David Herszenhorn, "With Stunts and Vigilante Escapades, a Populist Gains Ground in Ukraine," *New York Times*, October 24, 2014, http://www.ny- times.com/2014/10/25/world/europe/with-stunts-and-vigilante-escapades-a- populist-gains-ground-in-ukraine.html?_r=0

Rick Noack, "Why Ukrainian politicians keep beating each other up," *Washington Post*, August 14, 2014, https://www.washingtonpost.com/news/worldviews/wp/2014/08/14/why-ukrainian-politicians-keep-beating-each-other-up/

*Kyiv Post,* "Lyashko's party set to win seats with radical populism," September 25, 2014, http://www.kyivpost.com/article/content/kyiv-post-plus/lyashkos-party-set-to-win-seats-with-radical-populism-366002.html

Nikolas Kozloff, "Ukraine: Insider Oligarchs Derail Maidan Revolution," Huffington Post, February 27, 2015, http://www.nikolaskozloff.com/blog.htm?post=987073

Anton Shekhovtsov and Andreas Umland, "Ukraine's Radical Right," *Journal of Democracy*, July 2014, Volume 25, Number 3, p 58-63, https://www.academia.edu/7615988/Ukraines_Radical_Right

Richard Balmforth and Natalia Zinets, "Ukraine's 'pitchfork' populist could be wild card in new line-up," Reuters, October 19, 2014, http://news.yahoo.com/ukraines-pitchfork-populist-could-wild-card-line-142804429.html

Nikolas Kozloff, "Interview: What Can Be Expected From Ukrainian Right in the Midst of Political and Military Crisis?" Huffington Post, July 30, 2014, http://www.nikolaskozloff.com/blog.htm?post=964962

Nikolas Kozloff, "Welcome to Ukraine: Wild West of Populist Politics," Huffington Post, March 6, 2015, http://www.nikolaskozloff.com/blog.htm?post=987889

## CHAPTER 4: RISE OF THE FAR RIGHT

Conn Hallinan and Foreign Policy In Focus, "The Dark Side of the Ukraine Revolt," *The Nation*, March 6, 2014 http://www.thenation.com/article/dark-side-ukraine-revolt/

Anton Shekhovtsov, "Security threats and the Ukrainian far right," Open Democracy, July 24, 2012, https://www.opendemocracy.net/opensecurity/anton-shekhovtsov/security-threats-and-ukrainian-far-right

Volodymyr Ishchenko, "Ukraine has ignored the far right for too long – it must wake up to the danger," *Guardian*, November 13, 2014, http://www.theguardian.com/commentisfree/2014/nov/13/ukraine-far-right-fascism-mps

David Stern, "Svoboda: The rise of Ukraine's ultra-nationalists," BBC, December 26, 2012, http://www.bbc.com/news/magazine-20824693

"Ukraine's revolution and the far right," BBC, March 7, 2014, http://www.bbc.com/news/world-europe-26468720

"Svoboda party members in Ukrainian government resign – Deputy Premier Sych," Interfax, November 12, 2014, http://en.interfax.com.ua/news/general/234059.html

David Stern, "Ukraine underplays role of far right in conflict," BBC, December 13, 2014, http://www.bbc.com/news/world-europe-30414955

"Russian journalist interviews Azov commander Andrii Biletskyi," Euro-Maidan Press, December 17, 2014, http://euromaidanpress.com/2014/12/17/russian-journalist-interviews-azov-commander-andrii-biletskyi/

Krytyka Polityczna, "Vasyl Cherepanyn heavily beaten by paramilitary thugs," Political Critique, September 24, 2014, http://politicalcritique.org/archive/2014/vasyl-cherepanyn-heavily-beaten-by-paramilitary-thugs/

David Stern, "Ukraine crisis: Is conflict fuelling far-right threat?" BBC, September 8, 2015, http://www.bbc.com/news/world-europe-34176602

Michael Goldfarb, "Euro 2012: antisemitic echoes that threaten celebration of football," *Guardian*, June 2, 2012, http://www.theguardian.com/world/2012/jun/02/euro-2012-antisemitic-football

"Russian journalist interviews Azov commander Andrii Biletskyi," EuroMaidan Press, December 17, 2014, HTTP://EUROMAIDANPRESS.COM/2014/12/17/RUSSIAN-JOURNALIST-INTERVIEWS-AZOV-COMMANDER-ANDRII-BILETSKYI/

"Ukraine president honors priest with checkered Holocaust-era record," Jewish Telegraphic Agency, August 1, 2015, http://www.jta.org/2015/08/01/news-opinion/world/ukraine-president-honors-priest-with-checkered-holocaust-era-record

Vasyl Trukhan, "Poroshenko honours Ukraine Church leader derided by Russia," Agence France Presse, July 29, 2015, http://news.yahoo.com/poroshenko-honours-ukraine-church-leader-derided-russia-192601079.html

Sabra Ayres, "Shrouded by myth, Ukraine's past proves an obstacle to its future," *Christian Science Monitor*, December 4, 2014, http://www.csmonitor.com/World/Europe/2014/1204/Shrouded-by-myth-Ukraine-s-past-proves-an-obstacle-to-its-future

Tom Parfitt, "Ukraine's 'history laws' purge it of communist symbols but divide the population," *Telegraph*, June 30, 2015, http://www.telegraph.co.uk/news/worldnews/europe/ukraine/11674511/Ukraines-history-laws-purge-it-of-communist-symbols-but-divide-the-population.html

Patrick Cockburn, "To see what Ukraine's future may be, just look at Lviv's shameful past," Independent, March 8, 2014, http://www.independent.co.uk/voices/commentators/to-see-what-ukraines-future-may-be-just-look-at-lvivs-shameful-past-9178968.html

Nikolas Kozloff, "Ukrainian Diaspora Must Jettison Right Wing Tendencies," Huffington Post, August 17, 2015, http://www.nikolaskozloff.com/blog. htm?post=1006457

Nikolas Kozloff, "Does Ukraine Have an Anti-Semitism Problem?" al-Jazeera, November 18, 2014, http://www.nikolaskozloff.com/blog.htm?post=976832

Nikolas Kozloff, "Ukraine: Still Failing on World War II," Huffington Post, December 25, 2014, http://www.nikolaskozloff.com/blog. htm?post=979864

"Latest from OSCE Special Monitoring Mission (SMM) to Ukraine,"OSCE web site, August 19, 2014, http://www.osce.org/ukraine-smm/122847

## Chapter 5: Ukraine and Anti-Semitism Debate

Conn Hallinan and Foreign Policy In Focus, "The Dark Side of the Ukraine Revolt," *The Nation,* March 6, 2014, http://www.thenation.com/article/dark-side-ukraine-revolt/

Timothy Ash, "Many positives in today's Ukraine, but risk of deeper Russian intervention remains," *Kyiv Post,* October 31, 2014, http://www.kyivpost.com/opinion/op-ed/timothy-ash-many-positives-in-todays-ukraine-but-risk-of-deeper-russian-intervention-remains-370294.html

Central European Policy Institute, "CEPI Ukraine Watch," June 29, 2015, http://www.cepolicy.org/publications/cepi-ukraine-watch

Sam Sokol, "Election results buoy Ukrainian Jews," *Jerusalem Post,* October 27, 2014, http://www.jpost.com/Diaspora/Election-results-buoy-Ukrainian-Jews-379969

"The Virtual Library: Ukraine," Jewish Virtual Library Web site, https://www.jewishvirtuallibrary.org/jsource/vjw/ukraine.html#3

Nikolas Kozloff, "Interview: What Can Be Expected From Ukrainian Right in the Midst of Political and Military Crisis?" Huffington Post, July 30, 2014, http://www.nikolaskozloff.com/blog.htm?post=964962

Hannah Thoburn, "For the Kremlin, Ukrainian Anti-Semitism Is a Tool for Scaring Russians in Crimea," *Tablet*, March 7, 2014, http://www.tabletmag.com/jewish-news-and-politics/165263/ukraines-wedge-issue

Paul Berger, "Ukraine's Election Results Are Good for the Jews — But What Comes Next?," *Forward*, October 30, 2014, http://forward.com/news/208153/ukraine-s-election-results-are-good-for-the-jews/

"Pogroms," *International Encyclopedia of the Social Sciences*, 2008, http://www.encyclopedia.com/topic/Pogroms.aspx

"Ukraine," Yivo Encyclopedia of Jews in Eastern Europe, http://www.yivoencyclopedia.org/article.aspx/Ukraine

Richard Pipes, *Russia Under the Bolshevik Regime*, Vintage Books, New York 1994, 106

Vitaly Shevchenko, "Goodbye, Lenin: Ukraine moves to ban communist symbols," BBC, April 14, 2015, http://www.bbc.com/news/world-europe-32267075

"Modern Jewish History: Pogroms," Jewish Virtual Library Web site, http://www.jewishvirtuallibrary.org/jsource/History/pogroms.html

Patrick Cockburn, "To see what Ukraine's future may be, just look at Lviv's shameful past," Independent, March 8, 2014, http://www.independent.

co.uk/voices/commentators/to-see-what-ukraines-future-may-be-just-look-at-lvivs-shameful-past-9178968.html

Fred Weir and Monika Rębała, "Honors for Ukrainian nationalists anger their victims – in Poland," *Christian Science Monitor,* May 11, 2015, http://www.csmonitor.com/World/Europe/2015/0511/Honors-for-Ukrainian-nationalists-anger-their-victims-in-Poland

Josh Cohen, "Vladimir Putin calls Ukraine fascist and country's new law helps make his case," Reuters, May 14, 2015, http://blogs.reuters.com/great-debate/2015/05/14/putin-ties-ukraines-government-to-neo-nazis-a-new-law-seems-to-back-him-up/

"Ukraine's recognition of WWII nationalist group sparks Jewish concern," *Times of Israel* , May 23, 2015, http://www.timesofisrael.com/ukraines-recognition-of-wwii-nationalist-group-sparks-jewish-concern/

Leonid Bershidsky, "Nazis Triumph Over Communists in Ukraine," Bloomberg, May 19, 2015, http://www.bloombergview.com/articles/2015-05-19/nazis-triumph-over-communists-in-ukraine

"Ukraine crisis makes EU eastern partnership more important: Merkel," Reuters, May 21, 2015, http://www.reuters.com/article/us-ukraine-crisis-eu-merkel-idUSKBN0O612O20150521

Eduard Dolinsky, "On the Ukrainian president signing a law honoring WWII Ukrainian nationalists," *Jerusalem Post,* June 1, 2015, http://www.jpost.com/Opinion/On-the-Ukrainian-president-signing-a-law-honoring-WWII-Ukrainian-nationalists-404735

"Ukraine to Honor Groups That Killed Jews in World War II," *Haaretz,* May 21, 2015, http://www.haaretz.com/world-news/1.657381

Christopher Gilley and Per Anders Rudling, "The History Wars in Ukraine Are Heating Up," History News Network," May 9, 015, http://historynews-network.org/article/159301

# Chapter 6: Creating a New National Identity

David R. Marples, "Open Letter from Scholars and Experts on Ukraine Re. the So-Called 'Anti-Communist Law,'" Krytyka, April 2015, http://krytyka.com/en/articles/open-letter-scholars-and-experts-ukraine-re-so-called-anti-communist-law

Fred Weir and Monika Rębała, "Honors for Ukrainian nationalists anger their victims – in Poland," *Christian Science Monitor*, May 11, 2015, http://www.csmonitor.com/World/Europe/2015/0511/Honors-for-Ukrainian-nationalists-anger-their-victims-in-Poland

"In New York's Little Ukraine, tension mounts ahead of vote," PBS, March 15, 2014, http://www.pbs.org/newshour/bb/new-yorks-little-ukraine-tension-mounts-ahead-vote/

Mark MacKinnon, "Bypassing official channels, Canada's Ukrainian diaspora finances and fights a war against Russia," *Globe and Mail*, Feb. 26, 2015, http://www.theglobeandmail.com/news/world/ukraine-canadas-unofficial-war/article23208129/

Olena Lennon, "Ukrainian Politics Abroad," *Foreign Affairs*, March 17, 2015 https://www.foreignaffairs.com/articles/eastern-europe-caucasus/2015-03-17/ukrainian-politics-abroad

Tarik Cyril Amar and Per Anders Rudling, "Why the Revival of Nationalist Myths in Ukraine Should Alarm Us," History News Network, May 19, 2014, http://historynewsnetwork.org/article/155618

"Ukrainian diaspora in America out of touch," *Kyiv Post*, Jan. 21, 2010, http://www.kyivpost.com/opinion/letters/ukrainian-diaspora-in-america-out-of-touch-57627.html

Vic Satzewich, *The Ukrainian Diaspora* (New York: Routledge, 2002), page 207

John-Paul Himka, "War Criminality: A Blank Spot in the Collective Memory of the Ukrainian Diaspora," York University web site, http://www.yorku.ca/soi/_Vol_5_1/_HTML/Himka.html

"Poroshenko Compares Holodomor With War In East," Radio Free Europe, November 22, 2014, http://www.rferl.org/content/ukraine-holodomor/26705458.html

Natasha Bertrand, "Russian-backed rebels are re-writing one of Ukraine's worst massacres," *Business Insider*, April 29, 2015, http://www.businessinsider.com/russian-backed-rebels-are-re-writing-one-of-ukraines-worst-tragedies-2015-4

Nikolas Kozloff, "Note to Ukraine: Time to Reconsider Your Historic Role Models," Huffington Post, May 27, 2015, http://www.nikolaskozloff.com/blog.htm?post=997521

"Holodomor: Memories of Ukraine's silent massacre," BBC, November 23, 2013, http://www.bbc.com/news/world-europe-25058256

"Ukrainians commemorate victims of Holodomor famine," *Kyiv Post*, November 23, 2014, http://www.kyivpost.com/multimedia/photo/ukrainians-commemorate-the-victims-of-holodomor-372787.html

Olga Bielkova, "From Holodomor to Maidan: How the Kremlin 'Brotherly Love' Cost Ukraine Millions of Lives," Huffington Post, November 23, 2014, http://www.huffingtonpost.com/olga-bielkova/from-holodomor-to-maidan-_b_6208478.html

Nina Strochlic, "The Ukrainian Face Collector Launches an Exhibition in Kiev," Daily Beast, August 21, 2014, http://www.thedailybeast.com/articles/2014/08/21/the-ukrainian-face-collector-launches-an-exhibition-in-kiev.html

Nikolas Kozloff, "Ukraine: Still Failing on World War II," Huffington Post, December 25, 2014, http://www.nikolaskozloff.com/blog.htm?post=979864

Jochen Hellbeck, "Ukraine Makes Amnesia the Law of the Land," *New Republic,* May 21, 2015, https://newrepublic.com/article/121880/new-laws-ukraine-make-it-illegal-bring-its-ugly-past

Nikolas Kozloff, "Does Ukraine Have an Anti-Semitism Problem?" al-Jazeera, November 18, 2014, http://www.nikolaskozloff.com/blog.htm?post=976832

Nikolas Kozloff, "Interview: What Can Be Expected From Ukrainian Right in the Midst of Political and Military Crisis?" Huffington Post, July 30, 2014, http://www.nikolaskozloff.com/blog.htm?post=964962

Stephen M. Norris, "Shevchenko's 'Kobzar' Portrays Ukrainian Nationhood," *Moscow Times,* March 17, 2014, http://www.themoscowtimes.com/arts_n_ideas/article/shevchenko-s-kobzar-portrays-ukrainian-nationhood/496226.html

Nina Porzucki, "A 19th-century poet is a symbol of resistance in Ukraine," Public Radio International, "The World," March 10, 2014, http://www.pri.org/stories/2014-03-10/19th-century-poet-symbol-resistance-ukraine

Rachel Donadio, "Unfinished Revolution: The Artists Soldier On," *New York Times,* April 29, 2014, http://www.nytimes.com/2014/04/30/arts/design/ukrainians-turn-to-the-arts-in-a-time-of-upheaval.html?_r=0

Natalia Zinets and Timothy Heritage, "National hero Shevchenko fails to unite Ukrainians and Russians," Reuters, March 9, 2014, http://www.reuters.com/article/us-ukraine-crisis-shevchenko-idUSBREA280UJ20140309

Casey Michel, "The Last Time Ukraine was Truly Free," Roads and Kingdoms, undated article from 2014, http://roadsandkingdoms.com/2014/the-last-time-ukraine-was-truly-free/

Michael Malet, "Anti-Semitism and the Makhnovists," Libcom ("libertarian communism") web site, https://libcom.org/history/anti-semitism-makhnovists-michael-malet

"From Maidan To Berkut: A Ukraine Protest Glossary," Radio Free Europe, December 4, 2013, http://www.rferl.org/content/ukraine-protest-glossary-euromaydan/25190085.html

Adam Taylor and Terri Rupar, "A glossary of 32 words, phrases, people and places you should probably know when following Ukraine's crisis," *Washington Post*, March 5, 2014, https://www.washingtonpost.com/news/worldviews/wp/2014/03/05/a-glossary-of-the-31-words-phrases-people-and-places-you-should-probably-know-to-follow-ukraines-crisis/

"What is 5.10.", Kiev1 web site, April 5, 2014, http://kiev1.org/en/chto-takoe-5-10.html

Tatiana Serafin, "Will Parliamentary Elections Bring Ukraine Its Savior?" *Forbes*, October 26, 2014, http://www.forbes.com/sites/tatianaserafin/2014/10/26/will-parliamentary-elections-bring-ukraine-its-savior/#32e711062781

Nikolas Kozloff, "In Midst of War, Ukrainian Political Left Ponders Next Moves," Huffington Post, January 5, 2015, http://www.nikolaskozloff.com/blog.htm?post=980568

Ziemowit Szczerek, "Ukraine as the Latest Fashion," *Ukrainian Week*, March 10, 2014, http://ukrainianweek.com/Society/104469

"Ukraine crisis: What do the flags mean?" BBC, March 6, 2014, http://www.bbc.com/news/blogs-magazine-monitor-26465465

"Ukrainian far-right party upstages FIFA with visit to Zurich headquarters," World Jewish Congress, Oct 28, 2013, http://www.worldjewishcongress.org/en/news/ukrainian-far-right-party-upstages-fifa-with-visit-to-zurich-headquarters

Michael Goldfarb, "Euro 2012: antisemitic echoes that threaten celebration of football," *Guardian*, June 2, 2012, http://www.theguardian.com/world/2012/jun/02/euro-2012-antisemitic-football

## CHAPTER 7: PLIGHT OF ETHNIC MINORITIES

Vladimir Ryzhkov, "Russia's treatment of Crimean Tatars echoes mistakes made by Soviets," *Guardian*, November 25, 2014, http://www.theguardian.com/world/2014/nov/25/-sp-russia-crimean-tatars-soviet-ukraine

Sofia Kochmar, "The life of minorities in Ukraine, one year after protests began," CatholicNewsAgency, November 21, 2014, http://www.catholicnewsagency.com/news/the-life-of-minorities-in-ukraine-one-year-after-protests-began-90246/

Jacob Resneck and Oren Dorell, "Tatars of Crimea say they stand with Ukraine," *USA Today,* March 6, 2014, http://www.usatoday.com/story/news/world/2014/03/06/ukraine-economy/6090567/

Myroslav Marynovych, "How Ukraine Will Get Crimea Back," *New Republic*, May 7, 2014, https://newrepublic.com/article/117683/ukraine-will-get-crimea-back

Shaun Walker, "Crimean Tatars divided between Russian and Ukrainian promises," *Guardian*, March 17, 2015, http://www.theguardian.com/world/2015/mar/17/crimean-tatars-divided-between-russian-and-ukrainian-promises

"Russian Dual-Citizenship-Declaration Law Comes Into Force," Radio Free Europe, August 4, 2014, http://www.rferl.org/content/russian-bill-criminalize-hiding-of-dual-citizenship-comes-into-force/25479962.html

Ilaria Parogni, "By Misunderstanding Crimea, the West Is Pushing Russia Further Away," Huffington Post, April 15, 2015, http://www.huffingtonpost.com/ilaria-parogni-/misunderstanding-crimea-west-russia_b_7073322.html

Gabriela Baczynksa, "Russia or Ukraine? Crimean Tatars consider their own vote," Reuters, March 25, 2014, http://www.reuters.com/article/us-ukraine-crisis-crimea-tatars-idUSBREA2O1F320140325

Carl Skutsch (ed), *Encyclopedia of the World's Minorities* (New York: Routledge, 2005), page 1188

J. Otto Pohl, "The Deportation and Fate of the Crimean Tatars," International Committee for Crimea, http://www.iccrimea.org/scholarly/jopohl.html

Yitzhak Arad, *The Holocaust in the Soviet Union* (Lincoln: University Nebraska Press, 2009), page 211

Matthew Luxmoore "Despite return 'home' to Russia, Crimeans ambivalent one year on," al-Jazeera America, March 27, 2015, http://america.aljazeera.com/articles/2015/3/27/russia-crimeans-ambivalent-one-year-on.html

Palash Ghosh, "Ukraine Maidan: Tatars In Crimea Caught In a Complex Conflict With Ethnic Russians And Ukrainians," International Business Times, February 26, 2014, HTTP://WWW.IBTIMES.COM/UKRAINE-MAIDAN-TATARS-CRIMEA-CAUGHT-COMPLEX-CONFLICT-ETHNIC-RUSSIANS-UKRAINIANS-1558124

"From Maidan To Berkut: A Ukraine Protest Glossary," Radio Free Europe, December 4, 2013, http://www.rferl.org/content/ukraine-protest-glossary-euromaydan/25190085.html

"Crimean Tatar people came out to support Euromaidan," YouTube, December 16, 2013, https://www.youtube.com/watch?v=Y7EX1E0ZpC4

Alessandra Prentice, "Tensions high in Ukraine's Crimea as rival crowds gather," Reuters, February 26, 2014, http://www.reuters.com/article/us-ukraine-crisis-crimea-parliament-idUSBREA1P1JA20140226

Nikolas Kozloff, "Ukraine: What's the Role of Religion in Post-Maidan Milieu?" Huffington Post, March 26, 2015, http://www.nikolaskozloff.com/blog.htm?post=990295

"Tatars flee Crimea, fearing persecution," World War 4 Report, March 23, 2014, http://ww4report.com/node/13094

Michael Weiss, "Crimea's Tatars: Running Out of Time and Options," Real Clear World, March 28, 2014, http://www.realclearworld.com/articles/2014/03/28/crimeas_tatars_running_out_of_time_and_options-2.html

Jeffrey Veidlinger, "Before Crimea Was an Ethnic Russian Stronghold, It Was a Potential Jewish Homeland," *Tablet* magazine, March 4, 2014 http://www.tabletmag.com/jewish-news-and-politics/164673/crimea-as-jewish-homeland?all=1

"From slavery to freedom: Crimean Jews and Krymchaks celebrate Passover in a new country," *Kyiv Post*, April 15, 2014, http://www.kyivpost.com/article/content/ukraine-abroad/from-slavery-to-freedom-crimean-jews-and-krymchaks-celebrate-passover-in-a-new-country-343676.html

"Crimean Karaites to be recognized indigenous people of Crimea," QHA Crimean News Agency, June 24, 2014, http://qha.com.ua/en/politics/crimean-karaites-to-be-recognized-indigenous-people-of-crimea/131710/

"Landmarks in Ukraine: Karayim Kenasa," Sight Seen in Ukraine web site, http://ukraine.kingdom.kiev.ua/region/09/kyiv-kenasa_en.php

Ari Yashar, "Crimea's Karaites Back the Russians," Israel National News, May 7, 2014, http://www.israelnationalnews.com/News/News.aspx/180353#. VvXHfY-cHIW

Talia Lavin, "In Crimea, a Karaite community carries on, and welcomes Russia," Jewish Telegraphic Agency, March 26, 2014, http://www.jta. org/2014/03/26/news-opinion/world/in-crimea-a-karaite-carries-on-and-welcomes-russia

Tatiana Schegoleva, "Karaites of Crimea: History and Present-Day Situation in Community," Euro-Asian Jewish Congress, May 29, 2011, http://eajc.org/ page34/news24063.html

Clément Zampa, "Crimean Karaites hail Russian takeover," *Times of Israel*, May 7, 2014, http://www.timesofisrael.com/crimean-karaites-hail-russian-takeover/

"New Leader of Crimean Karaites to Seek Return of Simferopol Kenesa," Religious Information Service of Ukraine, June 17, 2013, http://risu.org.ua/en/index/ all_news/other_confessions/karaimstvo_small_ethnic_religions/52662/

Lily Hyde, "From slavery to freedom: Crimean Jews and Krymchaks celebrate Passover in a new country," *Kyiv Post,* April 15, 2014, http://www.kyivpost. com/article/content/ukraine-abroad/from-slavery-to-freedom-crimean-jews-and-krymchaks-celebrate-passover-in-a-new-country-343676.html

John Haines, "Kárpátalja: Europe's Next Crimea?" Foreign Policy Research Institute, April, 2014, http://www.fpri.org/article/2014/04/ karpatalja-europes-next-crimea/

"Geography," World Academy of Carpatho-Rusyn Culture, http://www. rusyn.org/rusyns-geography.html

"RUSYN SCHOOLS IN SUBCARPATHIAN RUS' – 10 YEARS!" World Academy of Carpatho-Rusyn Culture, http://www.rusyn.org/rusynschools10yrs.html

"Ethnography," World Academy of Carpatho-Rusyn Culture, http://www.rusyn.org/ethethnography.html

Michael Blain,"My country, Carpathia, was stolen," *Cleveland Jewish News*, May 2, 2014, http://www.clevelandjewishnews.com/opinion/op-eds/article_025ff4e0-d07c-11e3-bc87-001a4bcf887a.html

"Ukraine's Hungarian minority nervous as crisis rages," Agence France-Presse, March 4, 2014, http://www.globalpost.com/dispatch/news/afp/140304/ukraines-hungarian-minority-nervous-crisis-rages

"AHF Statement: Upheaval in Ukraine - Protecting the Forgotten and Repressed Hungarian Minority," American Hungarian Federation, February 28, 2014, http://www.americanhungarianfederation.org/news_transcarpathia_ukraine.html

American Hungarian Federation, "Hungarian Minority in Ukraine – 'Strengthen Ukraine by Strengthening Minority Rights,'" http://www.americanhungarianfederation.org/news_transcarpathia_ukraine3.html

American Hungarian Federation, "AHF Statement: The Plight of the Hungarian Minority in Transcarpathia," March 10, 2014, http://www.americanhungarianfederation.org/news_transcarpathia_ukraine2.html

"Hungarians under threat in the Lower Carpathians," Jobbik web site, http://www.jobbik.com/hungarians_under_threat_in_the_lower_carpathians

"Hungarian Fascists Want A Piece of Ukraine Too," *American Interest,* http://www.the-american-interest.com/2014/03/31/hungarian-fascists-want-a-piece-of-ukraine-too/

Mitchell A. Orenstein, "Putin's Western Allies," *Foreign Affairs*, March 25, 2014, https://www.foreignaffairs.com/articles/russia-fsu/2014-03-25/putins-western-allies

Jan-Werner Mueller, "Hungary's election offers some disturbing lessons for Europe," *Guardian*, April 9, 2014, http://www.theguardian.com/commentisfree/2014/apr/09/hungary-election-europe-prime-minister-viktor-orban

"Ukraine must observe community rights, says Orbán," Politics.Hu, May 15, 2014, http://www.politics.hu/20140515/ukraine-must-observe-community-rights-says-orban/

Jobbik: "The new Ukrainian government is chauvinistic and illegitimate" Jobbik web site, March 3, 2014, http://www.jobbik.com/jobbik_new_ukrainian_government_chauvinistic_and_illegitimate

"Mass number of Transcarpathian residents receive Hungarian passports," Uzhgorod.in web site, August 14, 2012, http://uzhgorod.in/en/news/2012/iyul/mass_number_of_transcarpathian_residents_receive_hungarian_passports_video

Daniella Cheslow, "Hungary Jews Fret as Vote Signals Shift to Right," *Jewish Daily Forward*, April 16, 2014, http://forward.com/news/world/196590/hungary-jews-fret-as-vote-signals-shift-to-right/?p=all

Carol Matlack, "Why Europe's Far Right Is Getting Cozy With Russia," Bloomberg, April 24, 2014, http://www.bloomberg.com/news/articles/2014-04-24/why-europes-far-right-is-getting-cozy-with-russia

Oleg Shynkarenko, "Alexander Dugin: The Crazy Ideologue of the New Russian Empire," Daily Beast, April 2, 2014, http://www.thedailybeast.com/articles/2014/04/02/alexander-dugin-the-crazy-ideologue-of-the-new-russian-empire.html

Anton Shekhovtsov, "Does the Hungarian and Polish far right anticipate Ukraine's downfall?" February 10, 2014, http://anton-shekhovtsov.blogspot.com/2014/02/does-hungarian-and-polish-far-right.html

Nikolas Kozloff, "Ukraine Crisis: Time for Thorough Overhaul of the International Left," Huffington Post, March 20, 2014, http://www.nikolas-kozloff.com/blog.htm?post=951341

Nikolas Kozloff, "Ukraine: What is the Position of Ethnic Minorities? An Activist Speaks," Huffington Post, December 19, 2014, http://www.nikolas-kozloff.com/blog.htm?post=979484

## CHAPTER 8: RELIGION AND CULTURAL CONSERVATISM

Iryna Chernysh, "Viktor Yanukovych will take part in the events dedicated to the 1025th anniversary of the Baptism of Russia today," Ukrainian National News, July 26, 2013, http://www.unn.com.ua/en/news/1234787-cogodni-v-yanukovich-vizme-uchast-u-zakhodakh-prisvyachenikh-1025-richchyu-khreschennya-rusi

"Ukrainian Museum Director Destroys Critical Painting Ahead Of President's Visit," Radio Free Europe, April 1, 2016 http://www.rferl.org/content/ukraine-art-destroyed-kuznetsov-kievan-rus-yanukovych/25058261.html

"Blacked Out in Ukraine: Larissa Babij in conversation with Nikita Kadan," *Guernica*, February 3, 2014, https://www.guernicamag.com/art/blacked-out-in-ukraine/

"Ukrainian Museum Director Destroys Critical Painting Ahead Of President's Visit," Radio Free Europe, April 1, 2016, http://www.rferl.org/content/ukraine-art-destroyed-kuznetsov-kievan-rus-yanukovych/25058261.html

"UKRAINE: Eight arrested in protest over a religiously and politically controversial painting destroyed by a Ukrainian museum director," Independent Television News, July 26, 2013, http://www.itnsource.com/shotlist/RTV/2013/07/26/RTV260713007/RTV260713007-831?v=1

Cyril Hovorun, "Christians in Ukraine: Ecumenism in the Trenches," Catholic World Report, March 4, 2014 http://www.catholicworldreport.com/Item/2970/christians_in_ukraine_ecumenism_in_the_trenches.aspx

Joshua Keating, "Russia Gets Religion," Slate, November 11, 2014, http://www.slate.com/articles/news_and_politics/foreigners/2014/11/russia_orthodox_church_will_vladimir_putin_eradicate_all_boundaries_between.single.html

Geraldine Fagan, "Putin is pushing the Patriarch to the brink," Catholic Herald, February 19, 2015, http://www.catholicherald.co.uk/issues/february-20th-2015/putin-is-pushing-the-patriarch-to-the-brink/

George Weigel, "Ukrainian Lessons for the West," *National Review,* November 17, 2014, http://www.nationalreview.com/article/392768/ukrainian-lessons-west-george-weigel?splash=

Victor Gaetan, "Ukraine's 'Maidan' Protests Are Spiritual as Well as Political," National Catholic Register, December 27, 2013, http://www.ncregister.com/daily-news/ukraines-maidan-protests-are-spiritual-as-well-as-political

Natalia Moussienko, "The Art of Revolution: Creativity and EuroMaidan," *Wilson Quarterly,* November 19, 2014, http://wilsonquarterly.com/stories/art-revolution-creativity-and-euromaidan/

"German Lizaveta, "Made in Maidan: Artwork From the Heart of Ukraine's Revolution," Vocativ, March 18, 2014, http://www.vocativ.com/culture/art-culture/made-maidan-artwork-heart-ukraines-revolution/

Gregory Sholette, "On the Maidan Uprising and 'Imaginary Archive' in Kiev," Hyper Allergic, July 16, 2014, http://hyperallergic.com/137799/on-the-maidan-uprising-and-imaginary-archive-in-kiev/

# Chapter 9: LGBT and Women

"THIS IS GAY PROPAGANDA: LGBT RIGHTS & THE WAR IN UKRAINE," Vancouver Queer Film Festival, http://queerfilmfestival.ca/films/this-is-gay-propaganda-lgbt-rights-the-war-in-ukraine/

Dimiter Kenarov, "Dashed Hopes in Gay Ukraine," *Foreign Policy*, January 19, 2015, http://foreignpolicy.com/2015/01/19/dashed-hopes-in-gay-ukraine-maidan-russia/

"Situation For LGBT People In Ukraine Worsened Over Last Year," Medium, May 20, 2015, https://medium.com/@Hromadske/situation-for-lgbt-people-in-ukraine-worsened-over-last-year-291b83265914#.vpk8ob79v

Soraya Sarhaddi Nelson, "For Poland's Gay Community, A Shift In Public Attitudes, If Not Laws," National Public Radio, June 25, 2015, http://www.npr.org/sections/parallels/2015/06/25/417446107/for-polands-gay-community-a-shift-in-public-attitudes-if-not-laws

Randy R. Potts, "Will Kiev's LGBT Pride Go Ahead?" Daily Beast, June 5, 2015, http://www.thedailybeast.com/articles/2015/06/05/will-kiev-s-lgbt-pride-go-ahead.html

"LGBT Rights Are Human Rights: Pride Under Threat in Ukraine," Amnesty International, June 4, 2015, http://blog.amnestyusa.org/europe/lgbt-rights-are-human-rights-pride-under-threat-in-ukraine/

Aditya Tejas, "Ukraine Gay Pride Parade Attacked With Stones, Smoke Bombs," International Business Times, June 6, 2015, HTTP://WWW. IBTIMES.COM/UKRAINE-GAY-PRIDE-PARADE-ATTACKED -STONES-SMOKE-BOMBS-1955426

Michael K. Lavers, "Ukrainian LGBT group's community center attacked," *Washington Blade*, September 3, 2015, http://www.washingtonblade. com/2015/09/03/ukrainian-lgbt-groups-community-center-attacked/

Randy Potts, "Ukrainian LGBT Leader, Taras Karasiichuk, Seeks U.S. Asylum," Daily Beast, September 30, 2015, http://www.thedailybeast.com/ articles/2015/09/30/ukrainian-lgbt-leader-taras-karasiichuk-seeks-u-s-aylum. html

Tom Balmforth, "Kyiv LGBT Hand-Holding Experiment Ends In 'Neo-Nazi' Attack," Radio Free Europe, July 24, 2015, http://www.rferl.org/content/ukraine-kyiv-lgbt-video-attack/27150912.html

Dimiter Kenarov, "Dashed Hopes in Gay Ukraine," *Foreign Policy*, January 19, 2015 http://foreignpolicy.com/2015/01/19/dashed-hopes-in-gay-ukraine-maidan-russia/

Steve Lee, "In post-revolutionary Ukraine, homophobia and oppression deepen," *LGBT Weekly*, January 21, 2015, http://lgbtweekly.com/2015/01/21/ in-post-revolutionary-ukraine-homophobia-and-oppression-deepen/

Bogdan Globa, "One year after Euromaidan: What's changed for gay rights?" *EU Observer*, https://euobserver.com/opinion/127984

Oleksiy Kuzmenko "Ukraine LGBT Activists Worry About Future," Voice of America News, July 3, 2015, http://www.voanews.com/content/ukraine-lgbt-activists-worry-about-future/2848680.html

Alec Luhn, "Gay couple kicked and pepper sprayed by far-right mob in Kiev," *Guardian*, July 23, 2015, http://www.theguardian.com/world/2015/jul/23/gay-couple-kicked-pepper-sprayed-far-right-mob-kiev-ukraine

Susie Armitage, "These Ukrainian Billboards Are Aiming To Combat Anti-LGBT Discrimination," Buzz Feed, May 7, 2015, http://www.buzzfeed.com/susiearmitage/these-ukrainian-billboards-are-aiming-to-combat-anti-lgbt-di#.lekZvKn67O

Agence France-Presse, "Ukraine eschews visa-free EU travel by blocking law to protect gay people," November 5, 2015, http://www.theguardian.com/world/2015/nov/05/ukraine-visa-free-european-travel-anti-gay-law

Palash Ghosh, "Ukraine Girls Really Knock Me Out: Women Playing Crucial Roles In Euro-Maidan Protests," International Business times, February 28, 2014, http://www.ibtimes.com/ukraine-girls-really-knock-me-out-women-playing-crucial-roles-euro-maidan-protests-1558508

"Filmmaker captures women's efforts in Ukraine," *Washington Post*, February 22, 2014, https://www.washingtonpost.com/posttv/world/filmmaker-captures-womens-efforts-in-ukraine/2014/02/22/2b853276-9bf8-11e3-8112-52fdf646027b_video.html

Liana Satenstein, "7 Women in Ukraine Share Their Stories From the Front Lines of the Revolution," *Elle*, February 27, 2014, http://www.elle.com/culture/career-politics/news/a19020/ukrainian-women-share-their-stories/

Rebecca Moss, "Women Stand at the Frontlines of the Euromaidan Protest in Kiev," *Elle*, February 21, 2014, http://www.elle.com/culture/career-politics/news/a24362/womens-opposition-euromaidan-protest-kiev/

Shaun Walker, "The New Suffragettes: Witness the bare-chested defiance of Femen," *Independent*, May 28, 2013, http://www.independent.co.uk/

voices/comment/the-new-suffragettes-witness-the-bare-chested-defiance-of-femen-8634988.html

Benjamin Bidder, "Kiev's Topless Protestors: 'The Entire Ukraine Is a Brothel'" *Spiegel*, May 5, 2011, http://www.spiegel.de/international/europe/kiev-s-topless-protestors-the-entire-ukraine-is-a-brothel-a-760697.html

"Femen close the office in Ukraine, but the work will not stop," *Українська правда*, August 27, 2013, https://translate.google.com/translate?hl=en&sl=uk&tl=en&u=http%3A%2F%2Fwww.pravda.com.ua%2Fnews%2F2013%2F08%2F27%2F6996762%2F

Joanna Lillis, 'We want a voice': women fight for their rights in the former USSR, *Guardian*, March 8, 2015, http://www.theguardian.com/world/2015/mar/08/fight-womens-rights-former-ussr-post-soviet-states

Marianna Grigoryan, 'Slowly, change is coming': life for women in the post-Soviet world *Guardian*, March 8, 2015, http://www.theguardian.com/world/2015/mar/08/women-post-soviet-world-profiles